THE
GOOD
MARRIAGE

GUIDE

*The Practical Way to
Improve your Relationship*

JOHN FARRELLY RPN, BA, MSc Psych, MBA, RCSI

First published 2007 by
Veritas Publications
7/8 Lower Abbey Street
Dublin 1
Ireland
Email publications@veritas.ie
Website www.veritas.ie

ISBN 978 1 84730 034 8

10 9 8 7 6 5 4 3 2 1

A catalogue record for this book is available from the British Library.

Designed by Colette Dower
Printed in the Republic of Ireland by Betaprint, Dublin

Veritas books are printed on paper made from the wood pulp of managed forests. For every tree felled, at least one tree is planted, thereby renewing natural resources.

CONTENTS

*This book is dedicated to all married couples
who form the bedrock of our society
through good times and bad.
Special thanks to my wife Laura
and two sons Aaron and Ben
who daily gift me their unconditional love.*

FOREWORD

Marriage is the bedrock on which stable family life is best located. In recent decades many European countries, and the United States and Britain in particular, have seen an explosion in the rate of marital breakdown with over 50 per cent of marriages now ending in divorce. Even in Ireland, although the divorce rate is relatively low, the marital breakdown rate is creeping upwards. Society has an interest in addressing this social problem from two perspectives. For the couples themselves marital breakdown is a source of unhappiness and self-blame with attendant risks of alcohol abuse, depression, poverty and a range of other psychological and social difficulties. However, for children, the most vulnerable of all, marital breakdown can have serious consequences that persist in later life with, among other things, relationship problems being replicated in the next generation.

Yet, try as some commentators may to predict the demise of marriage, this ancient social institution continues to attract members in their hundreds of thousands in all societies every year. Nobody entering marriage imagines the shattered wedding photo being replaced by the *decree nisi* on the mantelpiece. So the motivation to succeed is high.

Why do marriages break down and what can be done to prevent this? The answers to these questions are as myriad as they are complex. It is certain that expectations surrounding all relationships are higher now than ever before, partly driven by our instant access to the mass media. And it communicates a simplistic, idealised and at times trivialised image of the realities and problems that arise in all marriages.

These high and unrealistic expectations make it very difficult for those involved to contemplate solutions when marital problems do arise. ACCORD plays a central role in helping couples deal with these difficulties when they occur. The 10,000 clients that it assisted last year is testimony to the huge contribution that it is making to healing hurt couples as they struggle in their marriages.

The Good Marriage Guide not only debunks many of the misunderstandings about 'real marriage' but it vests married couples with skills necessary to understand and cope with the relationship problems that confront them. The range of difficulties that it covers is wide and these are based on real-life situations. An accessible and professional book such as this will greatly assist those who, in the first instance, wish to understand and self-manage their difficulties. For those who are receiving marriage counselling it will be an extremely useful adjunct. However, all those preparing for marriage should be encouraged to read it also, as its approach will prepare them for tribulations that arise even in the best of relationships.

Patricia Casey
Professor of Psychiatry, University College Dublin and Consultant Psychiatrist, Matermisericordiae University Hospital, Dublin

INTRODUCTION

The sum which two married people owe to one another
defies calculation. It is an infinite debt,
which can only be discharged through eternity.
JOHANN WOLFGANG VON GOETHE

Someone once said that marriage is the riskiest activity taken on by the greatest number of people in our society. In western society half of marriages are expected to end in divorce. This book is a compact, concise and informative guide for couples who want to save or strengthen their marriage and relationship. The content is based on over fifteen years' experience in relationship counselling and in mental health and social research. It aims to provide psychological and social insights that will enable readers to transform, consolidate and most importantly enjoy their marriage and relationship.

The main audience for this book is married couples and those interested in marriage. While it has to be acknowledged that there are other ways that people form couple bonds these days, this book is written based on the experiences of married couples. All the concepts and illustrations are about married couples or those planning to marry. I hope that readers who are in other kinds of relationships may benefit as well, though they will have to adapt what they read to their own situation.

The Good Marriage Guide is written in modern and accessible language. Too often when people attempt to find information to help their marriage they are confronted with professional jargon that is out of contact with the reality of modern living. This book is a resource that couples can build their marriage around. It can also be used to help couples deal with a specific problem that arises in their relationship. It examines the key challenges for couples and assists them in confronting and mastering the inevitable crises of life whilst maintaining the strength of their marriage. It looks at how couples need to behave towards each other and how best to understand difference, whilst providing nurturance and comfort to each other, satisfying their mutual need for independence and offering continuing encouragement and support.

There can be no doubt that the core social and personal challenge of our time is how to make loving, permanent marriage work for ourselves and our children. It is the married couple who provide the glue for society. No amount of public policy, education or economic reform will solve society's problems unless we understand how men and women can sustain permanent bonds that are good for them, their children and their communities. Over the last decades a sneaking unintended trend towards pathologising marriage has slowly gained momentum. Most people only receive support and guidance when their marriage and relationship gets into trouble. A lot of experts and policy makers have fallen into the fantasy trap of assuming that a marriage is either good or bad. If a couple do certain positive things a marriage will be good and conversely if they do not the marriage will be bad. We need to reframe our thinking on what is a good or bad marriage. We need to change our thinking from the metaphor of the 'thin line between a happy and unhappy marriage'. In happy couples, the thin line has been replaced by the circle. The marriage as circle has to learn to roll through good and bad times. All marriages, no matter how good, are exposed to external stress and the constant barrage of modern life. All marriages will have conflict and indeed all marriages will have a time when each individual may feel isolated, alone and at their wits' end.

The Thin Line Metaphor

Good Marriage

Bad Marriage

The Circle Metaphor

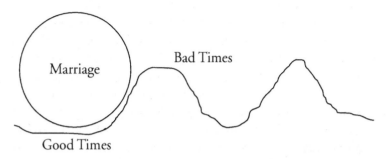

This book maps out the typical marriage journey showing that, in the process of marriage, conflict will be encountered many times. The trick is how we deal with it!

Chapter 1 introduces the reader to the concept of family of origin. This chapter makes readers aware that both they and their partner are not just people who have dropped complete into each other's lap, but instead are individuals who have been shaped by the family and environment in which they grew up. The reader will begin to understand how each partner views the world through their own particular family lens. This lens has been crafted, refined and in some cases even cracked by the experiences each person has in their family of origin. The family we grew up in had rules, regulations, codes of behaviour and certain ways of looking at the world. This chapter explains how each partner is actually a product of their family of origin; how we have to become aware of our own worldviews, perceptions and prejudices. The reader is given the psychological tools to examine their own family of origin, begin to understand their own perception of reality and crucially learn how to overcome any faulty thinking and perceptions that belong to childhood and are of no use in their present reality. The chapter sows the seeds that facilitate the reader to separate emotionally from their childhood so as to invest fully in the marriage and, at the same time, to redefine the lines of connection with both families of origin. This allows the couple to build togetherness based on mutual identification and shared intimacy, while at the same time setting boundaries to protect each partner's autonomy.

Love and commitment to the relationship are necessary for a marriage, but they are not enough. Good communication in marriage includes honest sharing of feelings, accurately sending and receiving messages, and empathy. It involves couples talking to each other more often, discussing personal topics more often, spending less time in conflict and showing a greater understanding and sensitivity to each other's feelings. Chapter 2 looks at the area of communication and more particularly how to communicate effectively with your spouse and family. Communication involves almost every aspect of our interactions with others. For this reason, communication and relationships are inseparable: you cannot have a relationship with someone without communicating with them. One of the greatest assets in any relationship is being able to communicate. Articulating your thoughts and being certain that your spouse understands what you wish to say take considerable practice. Often we believe we are saying one thing, while our partner is hearing something entirely different. Communication requires both good transmission skills (articulation) and good receptive skills (listening). Without both, communication will be difficult at best. This chapter helps couples to avoid the fatal trap where all too often the genuine warmth and concern that they have for each other gets lost in the murky world of perceptions and miscommunication.

Once the reader has an understanding of their personal history and how to communicate effectively we then move on to the specific area of conflict. Time and again couples come to my clinic appearing dizzy, dazed and confused, as though they have just gone ten rounds with Muhammad Ali. In reality they have spent the last few years in a confusing battle with their spouse. The kitchen or bedroom is the ring and the tools of the trade are insults, criticism, hurt and confusion. Chapter 3 sets out clearly how couples can avoid the draining, repetitive conflicts and fights that jump out of nowhere and leave both partners feeling confused and alone. Readers will learn that conflict is a part of life; it exists as a reality of any relationship and is not necessarily bad. In fact a relationship with no apparent conflict may be unhealthier than one with frequent conflict. Conflicts are critical events that can weaken or strengthen a relationship. They can be productive, creating deeper understanding, closeness and respect, or they can be destructive, causing resentment, hostility and separation. Every couple will have at least ten areas of disagreement, each of which involves conflict. Conflicts run all the way from minor, unimportant differences to critical fights. There are conflicts of needs, wants, preferences, interests, opinions, beliefs and values. The real test is how the conflicts get resolved, not how many occur. In this chapter we describe the simple steps the reader can take to deal with conflict and ensure their relationship stays healthy, mutually satisfying and intimate.

The greatest story never told is how hard it is to come to terms with the challenges of parenting while maintaining a healthy relationship. Chapter 4 looks at how to ensure your marriage stays intact following the birth of a child. Building on the insight gained about their family of origin the reader will begin to understand how the psychological move from being somebody's son or daughter to being a father or mother has to be negotiated effectively by both partners. The chapter works through some of the known problems for couples in this area, ensuring that they look after each other at this critical period. It highlights the need to balance the couple-centred marriage and child-centred marriage. The final section of this chapter examines the whole area of sex and intimacy: how people can lose their sex drive following the birth of a baby, the reasons behind this and most importantly how to get it back on track.

Most of us have certain assumptions about our marriage: we chose someone and the other person chose us; we have the same values and have decided to have an exclusive relationship; even though we may have some problems, we love each other and therefore we are safe. Infidelity is one of the most deeply wounding encounters in marriage. When we find out our partner has been unfaithful, everything we believe is totally shattered and we have to rebuild our world. The fact that infidelity is often unexpected and not part of our assumption about how a relationship operates causes traumatic reactions. Chapter 5 examines the area of infidelity, specifically why it happens, how to avoid it and how to rebuild a relationship following infidelity.

The fact that we now live in a computer and technology age is examined in detail in Chapter 6. No matter where we look, technology is changing and shaping our lives. Twenty years ago, computers, mobile phones and the modern information age did not exist. Now it is so pervasive that it warrants a chapter all to itself in this book. Whilst all of this has led to greater connectivity and ability to communicate, it has also created a context in which it can be hard to just stop and give time to your marriage and family. This chapter looks at how we have to ensure that we maintain time for our marriage and partner whilst living in this modern era. It then drills down to the three main areas where the internet is putting pressure on relationships: infidelity, pornography and gambling. These areas are addressed and solutions are offered to help couples avoid these pitfalls and regain balance in their relationship.

The challenge of work–life balance, a major challenge for all modern married couples, is the central theme of Chapter 7. Before couples can move forward they need to realise and figure out what work–life balance means to them. If couples can work out this conundrum, then their future life together will be dramatically better. In the modern age of results-driven living most workers need to be obsessive, work incredibly hard and generally end up maxed out. This manifests itself in many ways, including always being overcommitted, regularly being exhausted and having a marriage and home life that are squeezed into leftover time. This comes at a cost – no or low balance in life. Many married couples are on the road from Monday to Friday, arriving home exhausted at the end of the day. At weekends the modern couple sleeps a lot, spends time in front of the computer getting caught up on all the 'stuff they didn't get to during the week' and when they go out, are always tired and withdrawn. The burnout cycle continues year on year and creates an environment that is not conducive to a happy married and family life. This chapter looks at the whole area in detail and offers readers tips on how to create a healthy balance that favours family and married life.

The real secret to getting the most out of this book is for each partner to read it and pledge to change their own behaviour and thinking. It is essential to realise that personal change and growth is the key to developing a successful marriage. Good things in marriage don't happen without the effort of both partners. Couples need to avoid the modern trap of viewing marriage more as a 'contract' rather than a 'covenant' by revisiting marital vows, ensuring their marriage becomes their highest priority and making the time needed to keep it strong. Each couple needs to learn to work together unselfishly in building a relationship that will meet, as far as possible, the needs of both partners. They must be prepared to make all possible changes for the good of the marriage. Couples who stay together do what is necessary to make the marriage a happy one. They find out what brings their partner happiness and then do it often. They realise that not all times will be good and gain an insight into the everyday obvious pressures and also the psychological structures to ensure that the love that brought them together is strengthened over the lifetime of their marriage. This book facilitates that quest. It will help you, your spouse and your children to be part of a marriage and family that is good, balanced and enjoyable.

FAMILY OF ORIGIN
IN-LAWS, OUTLAWS
AND MOVING ON

CHAPTER 1

If you cannot get rid of the family skeleton,
you may as well make it dance.

GEORGE BERNARD SHAW

It sounds strange but separation, particularly psychological separation, is the key to developing and maintaining a strong marriage. This in essence means that both partners in a marriage have to separate emotionally from their childhood so as to invest fully in the marriage and, at the same time, to redefine the lines of connection with both families of origin. A specific example of the implications of family of origin is research which shows that how tied a husband is to his parents can make or break a new marriage. The researchers discovered this by surveying couples who were eighteen to thirty years old and had been married between six and thirteen months on how much they felt they were psychologically detached from their parents and had established themselves as distinct individuals. Each spouse was also asked whether they felt they got along as a couple, whether they were satisfied with the marriage, whether they received enough affection and whether they agreed enough on various issues.

A husband's lack of independence from both his parents was the biggest predictor for both spouses not adjusting very well to the new marriage. Both spouses reported higher levels of adjustment and satisfaction in their marriage when the husbands were free from excessive guilt, anxiety, mistrust, responsibility, inhibition, resentment and anger in relation to their mothers. The couples were also better adjusted in their new marriage when the husband possessed a greater ability to manage and direct practical affairs without the help of their fathers. Wives' adjustment to marriage seemed to depend on how well the husbands separated from their parents, whereas husbands' adjustment to marriage depended on how well both spouses separated from their parents' influence.

Wives can also become enmeshed in communication and structures that have developed in their family of origin. Research by Gottman, Katz and Hooven (1999) indicates that women who grow up in punitive and emotionally dismissive families or in an invalidating environment tend to dismiss their own emotions in adulthood. Another example is the finding that parents-in-law who are high in expressed emotion can have a destabilising and intrusive effect on the new married couple and their family. It can be hard to put boundaries on the behaviour of a parent who is volatile. Very often the new family begins to form around the behaviour of the unbalanced parent from the family of origin.

A lot of things affect the type of family of origin we come from, particularly:

- Parents' education
- Family's social class or economic status
- Parents' relationship with their own parents
- Culture (extended family influence) and exposure to other cultures
- Sibling relationships
- Faith – family's active or non-active participation
- Divorce and separation
- Illness and addictions.

When the above dynamics are blended together, we tend to have a number of possible ways of viewing a family of origin:

1. **Close knit family** – they love each other and socialise around each other. There is regular direct face-to-face contact as well as quick communication via phone, e-mail etc. However, in general, each family member knows when to draw the line.
2. **Loosely knit family** – they love each other, but do not socialise with each other so much. Family members will call each other at their convenience.

3. **Enmeshed family** – they are too close, do not know when to let go and when to draw the line. There is over involvement of the family in individual issues and relationships.

4. *Laissez-faire* **family** – there are loose bonds; siblings and parents forge individual lives with very little communication and rare socialisation. It can appear that family members do not care about each other.

So we grow up in our family of origin with its own particular shape, circumstances and worldview. The first relationship we observe is that of our parents. This forms a template deep in our unconscious that affects our future choice of partner. Our parents form a model of what relationships are like and what adult males and females are about. As such, these early imprints have a profound effect on our choice of mate and our expectations with respect to a relationship. If this early imprinting was positive, we are likely to have satisfying interpersonal relationships and a positive image of others. However, if it was negative, it may well have the opposite effect. Sometimes the effect was so negative, even though we may not be aware of it, that it can severely interfere with our interpersonal satisfaction. Repeated destructive relationships, co-dependence and generally unhealthy relationships may ensue. In these cases, professional intervention may be necessary before you can proceed with some of the steps outlined in this book. If in doubt, seek the help of a qualified professional trained in relationship skills.

A good example of how traces of the past sit in our minds was given by Sigmund Freud (Strachey, 1966), who cites the magic writing pad of our childhood days. We all remember 'Etch a Sketch', the toy board that you could draw on and then, as if by magic, erase the picture and begin again. As happens to most toys at some stage we get bored and rip it apart to see how the magic works. On the carbon underneath we see traces of all the drawings – and yet we thought that we had wiped them away. The human mind works in a similar way. Traces of all the encounters and experiences we have in our life are stored in the back of our minds. Over time experiences repeat themselves and before we know it some traces are bigger and more prominent than others. These traces are the building blocks of what we call our psychological worldview. Then, in the blink of an eye, these traces take on a power of their own. They begin to shape, create and alter how we see the world. Experiences and events that fit and add to these traces we notice and are drawn to; conversely, those that do not tally with this worldview often go unseen or cause us psychological distress.

These traces, built up during childhood, are suitable for the child's world, or for your role as son, daughter, brother or sister within your family of origin. However, many of these traces, evident in our behaviour, thoughts and attitudes towards our spouse, are not useful in adult life. They can choke and suffocate a marriage. The task for each partner is to think deeply about their behaviour and worldview; become aware of the repetitive traces and decide if they are worth having as part of their adult worldview and current love relationship or if they are a hindrance. Only the individual can decide to track and tackle their own traces. It is pointless to try to tackle your partner's traces unless you are aware of and have worked on your own.

People have great difficulty understanding how patterns, fights and ruptures can occur. One minute they are walking happily down the aisle and then, before they know it, their marriage seems to be falling apart. Very often this can be because spouses are interacting based on thoughts and emotions that belong to their role within their family of origin. I want to give you some basic understanding of how you can identify some of the patterns you may have experienced with your families of origin and are now unknowingly repeating in your new relationship. These can also occur in adulthood with your aging parents, your children or any other relationship where an out-of-date trace is rerun.

A simple example of this is whether you grew up in a family with high or low expressed emotion levels. High expressed emotion is where all things are spoken about, where all feelings are put on the table and where strong emotions are part and parcel of everyday interaction. Low expressed emotion is the opposite: here behaviours are more guarded; it is not acceptable to speak openly on all topics. Instead events are handled in a guarded matter-of-fact fashion. Now imagine if two people get married who come from these very different perspectives. What is comfortable for one partner can cause extreme anxiety for the other. This is not one spouse being antagonistic or troublesome – they are just acting in a way that is normal for them. To ensure satisfaction both spouses have to come out of their comfort zone, whilst at the same time learning to accept that the behaviour of their partner is not an offensive action.

To separate out from our family of origin each of us has to accomplish two major psychological tasks – separation and individuation. These are normal and healthy phases of human development. They are psychological processes that begin in the first year of life and are reworked throughout childhood, adolescence and adulthood. Separation relates to personal autonomy, independence, self-assertion and freedom of choice. It is characterised in early childhood by the use of the word 'No'. When a two year old says 'No' to their mother, they are exercising their inborn strivings to separate from the mother. Individuation relates to identity, uniqueness, having your own interests, points of view, likes and dislikes. It is characterised in early childhood by the words 'me' and 'mine'. It is also an inborn striving for children and, like separation, can either be aided and fostered by parents or thwarted and considered bad by parents. Dysfunctional families often punish both these struggles in their children. Often those who choose to separate and individuate are seen as traitors to the family. Health, growth, financial progress even sobriety can all be seen as moving too far away from the culture of the family of origin. Individuation, i.e. having your own identity and point of view, can be perceived by some families as a rejection of them. I have often seen people who have become successful, psychologically evolved and healthy being rejected by their families of origin. They are seen to have abandoned the family by those who have a hard time with separation; they are treated as if they have devalued and degraded the family by those who have greater difficulty with individuation. It is important that you think carefully about your ability to say 'No'. If this is not developed in each of the partners in a marriage then, over time, the relationship will become unbalanced and one partner will grow too dependent on their spouse or, even worse, the marriage will become dependent on outside influences or, worse again, will meander down a road to unhappiness.

Boundaries

One way of moving from your family of origin is to consciously construct boundaries of well-being. Boundaries are barriers that protect us and our marriage. There are two main types of boundaries: rigid and diffuse. If you have rigid boundaries, then barriers may exist that keep you from having meaningful relationships and understanding with your spouse. People who have rigid boundaries can become isolated or withdrawn from others, which can cause relationships to suffer. A diffuse boundary is the opposite of a rigid boundary: people with diffuse boundaries do not have clear, definable boundaries with others, and such individuals can have problems defining who they are. In situations where diffuse boundaries and a lack of individuation and separation exist within a family, it is common to find family over-involvement in the individual's life and marriage. This degree of understanding or accommodation between family members can be characterised by a loss of independence by one or all involved family members. This over-involvement is usually reflected by parents and in-laws who maintain and in some instances become increasingly over-dependent on each other at the expense of relationships outside the family of origin.

In this over-protective or enmeshed family example, empathy for each person within the family is so great that it allows an individual to 'feel' what the other or others within the family are experiencing. These behaviours occur when individual boundaries break down. This empathy is unhealthy, as it does not allow development without dependence. This causes the family to exclude other outsiders from having meaningful relationships with individuals within the family, often leading to frustration for the spouse, who is left outside and can very often be viewed as an outlaw because they will not accept the over-involvement of their spouse's family of origin. In a way, the diffuse or 'soft' boundaries within the family of origin cause the family unit's boundaries to become more rigid to outside-the-family relationships. This serves to increase the family's dependence on each other and allows the destructive behaviour to continue.

As with most things, there exists a happy medium. This happy medium is defined by having stable, healthy boundaries that allow for personal and meaningful relationships with others. A person with healthy boundaries is able to have a solid sense of self along with feelings of belongingness to their family as well as to their partner and others outside the family. Marrying our spouse means we turn our loyalties to them. That does not mean we are not loyal to our parents, but that we place priority on our husband or wife. One obvious step to leaving our parents that shows we place priority on our spouse is changing homes. Our attentions and efforts turn towards our new family's well-being and happiness and a calm, loving home. Here's an example:

> Janet and Tim had been married for a year when her mother complained about her daughter's situation. 'You're just wasting your money living in that apartment,' she began, 'and besides, that's no place to have children. When are you going to have children, anyway?'
>
> Janet didn't want to be disrespectful to her mother, but she and Tim had already discussed their wants and needs concerning their home and having children. They were happy in their apartment and wanted to wait a few more years before having children.
>
> When Tim walked through the door, Janet told him about the discussion with her mother. 'Maybe Mammy is right,' she said. Tim became angry. 'It's none of her business! It's not her life; it's our life!'
>
> The two argued for several hours. Janet felt she needed to defend her mother, and Tim felt disrespected by being told what he and his family should do.

It is important to mention that Janet's mother said those things because she loved her daughter. She wasn't trying to meddle or intrude – but she did. Janet would have best served her marriage by politely telling her mother that she and Tim made decisions together and, though she appreciated her mother's concern, in order to protect her marriage she had to ensure their independence and freedom to choose for themselves.

The Middle-Man Rule

One primary difficulty married couples face is managing conflict with the parents of their spouse. It is a very good idea to make your spouse the 'middle man' for conflicts you have with their parents. Relationships are stronger when they have time behind them and, as they say, blood is thicker than water. Therefore, in-laws will probably react better to a request from their son or daughter. If her parents need to back off, for example, its better that it comes from her.

> Jim and Laura lived about twenty miles from his parents. Many times, on weekends, Jim's parents would drive to their house and the four would play cards or chat. After several months of this, both Jim and Laura wanted to spend a weekend at home alone. 'Why can't we go to a film or go out for a meal or something by ourselves?' Laura asked.

If Laura had gone to Jim's parents, they might have been offended when she said she and Jim wanted time alone. They may have felt she forced Jim into siding with her. It could even be that because of this, they resented Laura for the rest of their lives. If, on the other hand, Jim went to his parents and told them he and Laura loved them very much but needed some time to do things by themselves, they would probably react with much more understanding and patience. It is important to be sensitive to your spouse's feelings concerning your parents. If they feel crowded or disrespected, it is important you take these feelings seriously and act to improve the situation. These principles should also be taken into consideration by parents and should influence the way they treat their child's spouse.

Independent Identity

You will know you are in a situation where change should occur when you and your spouse do not feel you have your own identity. One of the purposes of marriage is for a couple to establish an identity that is independent of their parents. If this does not happen, a healthy marriage becomes much more of a challenge. Some marriage experts say couples should not live in the same town as either of their parents. The reasoning is that with the constant availability of their parents, the couple does not learn to rely on each other. It's difficult to form an identity together unless each of you learns to rely on the other instead of parents. It is not my opinion that every couple should live in a separate town from their in-laws, but for some, that situation might be best. It might be better for you, for example, if your in-laws are too involved in certain aspects of your relationship – especially if they are too involved in conflicts between you and your spouse. Part of what it means to have your own identity as a couple is that conflicts are resolved without the involvement of in-laws. The scenario below shows ways a couple could fall into the trap of 'in-law dependence' and the consequences they might face if independence is not a priority.

> After six months of marriage, Eileen and Steve had their first big fight. What was the subject? It doesn't matter!
>
> While in tears, Eileen called her mother and told her about the entire ordeal. Her mother listened and became angrier by the minute. 'I'm coming over there,' her mother said.
>
> When she arrived at the couple's home, she immediately began telling Steve why Eileen was correct and scolded him for disagreeing. According to her, Steve owed Eileen an apology.
>
> From that point on, Steve had difficulty trusting his mother-in-law. He felt she plotted against him and wanted to control him. He also felt betrayed by his wife. He felt that she, rather than being on a team with him, called for backup to defeat him.

If you and your spouse are arguing about any subject, neither has the right to involve a parent in the disagreement. If your spouse brought a parent in on an argument, you would probably feel just as Steve did. You would feel it was 'them against you'. This violates the attitude of oneness that should exist in your marriage and relationship.

Mutual Respect

In all things, respect your mother-in-law and father-in-law. Remember, they are the parents of someone very special – your spouse. If you are a parent of a married child, your son-in-law or daughter-in-law is very special because they are your child's life partner. That said, it is best for each family to realise the independence of the other. Your spouse must know your parents will not interfere with the family you are building. Your parents must realise you and your spouse need to build a life and relationship separate from them. This requires patience and, at times, may be painful. It is important to honour and respect your in-laws, but above that, protect your marriage. This principle will pay great dividends in the future.

Here are a few ideas to help you in the process:

- *Make peace with your past*
  Recognise and accept the patterns that existed in your family of origin. Marriage is difficult enough without bringing those kinds of problems in with you. Some of your relationships may require much deeper healing than others. Whether or not reconciliation is possible for you, make the effort to make peace with your past. Then you will truly be able to make a fresh start with your new spouse.

- *Remember: You are not your parents!*
  While you need to be aware of repeating the mistakes of your parents and appreciate the structures and repetitions of your family of origin, it is also important to remember that you are not your parents! Sure, you share many of the same strengths and weaknesses, but you have the power to make different decisions.

- *Remember: Your spouse is not your parents, either!*
  On the flip side, it is also very easy to begin to equate your spouse with your parents. We keep one eye on them at all times, expecting them to make the same mistakes our parents made at any moment. This is often rooted in a person's disbelief that a happy marriage is possible – 'If it is not me that will mess it up, it will be my spouse!'

- *Learn from your past*
  It is often said that those who don't learn from history are condemned to repeat it. If you don't want to repeat the mistakes of your parents, learn from them! Where did they go wrong? What decisions, behaviours and beliefs led them to contentment or conflict? What protections can you build into your marriage to ensure that you don't go down that road?

You can also look for good role models. Is there someone you know who has the kind of marriage that you want to have? Maybe it's your spouse's parents, a friend or another relative. Observe how they interact and ask them what their secret is. It is always a good idea to draw on the wisdom of others.

- *Build a better future*
  Your past should not dictate who you are, but it should impact who you become. When dealing with past hurts there are two temptations: to wallow in them or to bury them. In the first case, we get stuck in the past and find ourselves unable to move on; in the latter, we deny the events ever happened and miss out on the learning experience. Hurts in families can last for years and even be passed on down through generations cutting both wide and deep. Perhaps you are familiar with the 'I haven't talked to my sister since I left home at eighteen' or the 'No one invites Uncle Jack after he ran Dad's business into the ground twenty-three years ago'. In your marriage and relationship have the strength to move on from the past and concentrate on what is good for you, your spouse and your children.

Finally, it is important to remember that each partner comes with some good and some bad family-of-origin traits. However, very often, rather than admit the dysfunctional part of our own family-of-origin traits, we spend a lot of time pointing out the dysfunction in our spouse's family of origin: 'Your family must not love each other because they don't call each other'; 'You are all too close and getting too much into my business'; 'You can talk to your family about yourself, but please not about me or the kids'. It is important to recognise the patterns that worked when you were at home with your parents but do not work with your spouse because of their experience. Recognise that your spouse and children come before your parents and siblings. While it is difficult to recognise and change habits formed while growing up we need to recognise the areas in our upbringing that are adversely affecting our marriage and family. It is hard work overcoming family-of-origin issues; however, once this work is done it can set a solid foundation for the future.

COMMUNICATION AND HEALTHY RELATIONSHIPS

*Sticks and stones are hard on bones
aimed with angry art,
words can sting like anything
but silence breaks the heart.*

SUZANNE NICHOLS

Time and time again the major complaint I hear from couples is that their partner is not communicating well or that communication has broken down. Communication involves almost every aspect of our interactions with others; for this reason, communication and relationships are inseparable. You cannot have a relationship with someone without communicating with them. Being able to communicate is one of the greatest assets in any relationship. Being able to articulate your thoughts and being certain that your spouse understands what you wish to say take considerable practice.

We communicate by expressing our thoughts, ideas and feelings to others. We also communicate attitudes, values, priorities and beliefs. No matter what we actually say to our partner in words, we also send messages about what we think of them, what we think of ourselves and whether or not we're being sincere and genuine in what we say. Our non-verbal communication – those things we say with our gestures, facial expressions, tone of voice and attitude – speak volumes. What we say and do, and how we say and do it, directly shapes how our partner and family experience us. In fact, many times, the opinions people form about us are based on the way we communicate, and this in turn directly influences how they communicate in response. In other words, *communication is a two-way street*. It can be clear or vague, open or guarded, honest or dishonest – it can even be spoken or non-spoken – but there is no such thing as 'non-communication'. In fact, virtually everything we do in the company of our spouse communicates something.

Because our ideas and interests are transmitted through the way we communicate, we are more likely to get our needs met if we are effective communicators. The problem is that often we think we are communicating one thing but are actually communicating something quite different, or we are communicating so poorly that no one quite understands what we are trying to say. While there are many factors involved in healthy relationships, the ability to communicate effectively is one important route to mutual satisfaction. Simply put, there are two ways to communicate with others: effectively and ineffectively.

Ineffective communication is characterised by one or more the following elements:

- **Indirect** (doesn't get to the point, never clearly states purpose or intention)
- **Passive** (timid and reserved)
- **Antagonistic** (angry, aggressive or hostile)
- **Cryptic** (underlying message or purpose is obscured and requires interpretation)
- **Hidden** (true agenda is never stated directly).

On the other hand, effective communication is:

- **Direct** (to the point, leaving no doubt as to meaning or purpose)
- **Assertive** (not afraid to state what is wanted or why)
- **Congenial** (affable and friendly)
- **Clear** (underlying issues are clear)
- **Open** (no intentionally hidden messages or meanings)
- **Verbal** (words are used to clearly express ideas)
- **Two way** (equal amounts of talking and listening)

- **Responsive** (attention paid to the needs and perspective of the other person)
- **On track** (correctly interprets responses and needs of the other person)
- **Honest** (true feelings, thoughts and needs are stated).

As you can see, it is easier to be a bad communicator than a good one!

Think about the first time you met your spouse; how you made certain that your communication was effective so that you would grab their attention. Have a look at the list above and you will see that you mainly used the list of effective communication skills. More than likely, you already have the skills to communicate well with your spouse – you just need to start using them again. Once you relearn these skills and begin practising them, they will help you not just in your marriage, but in all aspects of your life. Effective communication is essential in day-to-day life, and especially so in important relationships.

It must be recognised that as we become comfortable and safe in a relationship we can become lazy in our communication. Think of how you used to communicate to your siblings or parents. Very often communication in families of origin develops its own code but ultimately drifts towards the ineffective end of the scale. It is amazing to view couples communicate to each other in an ineffective manner. Many do not realise that they are treating and speaking to their partner in a way that would not be accepted if they were speaking to a person outside of the relationship. This boils down to the human tendency to treat the person they love the most and feel most secure around in a tardy fashion. Because we feel secure we do not make the same effort to communicate as we would in a novel or unknown situation. Think of a young child: they will not shout and scream at a stranger; instead they will direct their anger at the person they love the most, usually the mother. Married people need to become aware of this human tendency and at all times be on their guard against it. My experience with couples has lead to the formulation of the ideal template for communication within a marriage, specifically:

- **Put a premium on openness**. Find ways to be honest, express your feelings and share ideas.
- **Share your problems**. Sharing the good times and the bad times is important in relationships. It serves to deepen and strengthen relationships and communication within them.
- **Share your daily life**. Share those things in your life that are mildly interesting, funny, sad or affect you in some way. Find a way to connect with your spouse, sharing your life with them and allowing them to share their lives with you.
- **Avoid verbally bruising your spouse**. Refrain from insults, put-downs and expressions of disgust. Avoid generalisations – they are stereotypes and can cause hurt.
- **Boost self-esteem, don't crush it**. When it comes to relationship building, naming your partner's deficiencies or failures is rarely as effective as praise. Focus on one another's positive traits. Find something good to say, catch each other doing something right and help build self-confidence and self-esteem.
- **Avoid controlling**. Whenever one partner seeks to always be right, always be the agenda-setter and always be the virtuous one, they may feel like a winner, but it's the relationship that loses.

As stated above, a key point is to remain on guard against taking one another for granted. This can be a killer for a relationship. It usually occurs sometime after the honeymoon period, when our partner feels taken for granted, not respected or acknowledged, and feels that others are a higher priority. If this starts to happen, resentment brews. A regular communication check-in with your spouse as to how they are feeling about the relationship can help avert resentment build-up. There are two types of meeting that can facilitate communication: a business meeting and a date night. Couples often find that scheduling regular business meetings, just as one would conduct in a business partnership, to discuss the business of the marriage is helpful and indicates that the marriage is a high priority in their life. Date night is one evening each week set aside for the purpose of emotional connecting. No business matters are discussed. Each partner takes responsibility on alternative weeks for planning the date, just as they might have done during courtship. Dates do not have to be elaborate events – a picnic on the bedroom floor or a walk in the local park at sunset can be every bit as romantic as a €200 dinner.

Maintaining the romance in a relationship is vital to the vibrancy of the relationship. Once people marry they can become quite lax in this department. They allow business, household tasks and children to get in the way of their romantic life. In a busy life, especially if there are children, it takes considerable effort to maintain romance. It takes planning, creativity and commitment, but it is worth it.

The following are two of the key factors that couples want in their relationship:

- **Compliments**. It costs nothing to compliment your partner and it really feels good to receive them. We are often slow about paying compliments to our spouse, letting them know that we think they are pretty/handsome, smart, clever, well-dressed, kind, a good parent etc. We do not have to wait until some occasion when we purchase a greeting card to let our partner know that we think they are special. If we do not compliment each other then who will? It is not just something we should try to do but instead it is an essential behaviour for a successful relationship. Your spouse chose you because when they were with you they felt a positive mirroring of themselves. They felt alive, respected and loved. If this ceases what is the point in being together? After all, we can find plenty of people to put us down and make us feel bad but very few who can go beneath and compliment us just for being ourselves.

- **Appreciation**. Appreciation is a predisposition, an inclination, openness and readiness of the heart to notice the person who has chosen us and to sense that our chosen relationship is an awesome thing, not to be taken lightly or for granted. An attitude of appreciation colours our perception of our relationship and everything that happens within it. Thanking your partner for making dinner or taking out the rubbish, picking up clothes from the dry-cleaners and in general letting them know that they are appreciated can go a long way towards creating a caring environment. Couples are very quick to criticise one another when tasks do not get done, but they can be very remiss when it comes to showing appreciation.

The above two points are based on the psychological process of reciprocation. If human beings are given a gift or shown appreciation it initiates a 'click-whirr' process in the brain. In other words, it creates an automatic response in us. Instead of constantly looking at your partner's negative side, try using the reciprocation rule and watch what happens. One very simple way to use this rule is by doing an 'appreciation letter'.

'Doing' an Appreciation Letter

Appreciation letters are so simple that it's a wonder to me that the world isn't overflowing with them. The soft language of approval and gratitude wrapped in a letter that is intimate and special is a powerful way of appreciating your partner. Try writing an appreciation letter to your partner – I guarantee you they will respond and reciprocate your love!

Use these steps:

- Think of a special name, past or present, that only you call your spouse; use this special name in the letter.
- Begin the letter with the simple words:
  'I appreciate you because …'

- Tell your partner the special things you notice about them.
- Using the following words to start sentences tell your partner how empty your life would be without them:
  'Without you in my life I would feel …'

- End the letter by simply saying, 'I love you'.
- Finally, but this is the most important step, place the letter on your partner's pillow or, for even more surprise, post it to them.

Wait and watch what happens. You will be surprised how quickly your partner reciprocates!

As you will know, maintaining a contemporary marriage is no easy task. It requires hard work. To think that a successful marriage – a relationship between two people that is fulfilling, enhancing of one's sense of self-esteem, emotionally gratifying, nurturing and supportive – can be achieved by merely living under the same roof without investing effort and time is very naive. Some individuals believe that marriage should be easy and if it is not, they think something is wrong. Marriage, like any other worthwhile endeavour, requires patience and practice. When there is difficulty, it may require outside help. Just as a business may require a consultant, so too might a marriage. Today's relationships are complex and dynamic entities that become even more complex as children enter the picture, for then there are additional dynamics that must be incorporated into the mix. Maintaining a long-term relationship is one of our most significant challenges.

Based on my work with thousands of couples I would offer the following broad advice. Before and whilst communicating, it is important to learn to think before you speak. The ability to bite your tongue before that provocative remark comes out of your mouth can often help in avoiding a huge fight. Take your time and listen. Try to understand what your partner is saying and, more importantly, ensure your partner's voice is recognised. If you are a talker try to create boundaries and set limits on your need to speak. You know how much verbal contact you and your partner can take and how much will ignite your internal nuclear bomb. Try to avoid overreacting, as this tends to escalate into all-out wars. Don't do it!

Active Listening Exercise
If you and your spouse feel you need to work on communication, try the following steps:

- Arrange for a convenient meeting time rather than trying to have a discussion on the fly when it is likely to be interrupted.
- Find a 'talking stick' (any small object will do). So long as one person is holding the stick, that person also holds the floor. Once the stick is passed, it becomes the other person's time to talk. This technique prevents interruptions.
- Express your point and then, passing the stick, ask your spouse to repeat what you said so that you can be certain that you were at least heard. If your partner is not able to repeat what you said or you do not feel understood, repeat your point until you are satisfied.
- The listener's job during this exercise is to be certain you understand and communicate that understanding to your spouse before you comment on the content of what you are being told.
- Once your partner feels heard, then it becomes your turn to comment and be heard.
- Continue this process until you come to a resolution, passing the 'talking stick' and alternately being in the role of transmitter and receiver.

Once learned this 'active listening' approach can prevent misunderstandings and serve to keep emotions under control. It is difficult to react emotionally if you are truly listening and have to communicate understanding before you get a chance to react.

Positive Communication
All communication is not positive. This is life. The real trick is to ensure that the positive communication outweighs the negative in your marriage. Good, warm, soft communication enhances self-esteem and self-worth and creates a climate of intimacy. However, enhancing intimacy starts with self-assessment. Consider your interactions with your partner. How often are you experiencing positive moments with your partner? How often are you creating positive moments in the relationship? How often do you tell your partner what you appreciate about them and the relationship? How

often do you express gratitude for anything your partner does to contribute to your and the relationship's well-being? Even if you believe no one needs to be thanked for taking out the rubbish or doing the dishes, thank them anyway – we all need to be appreciated. How often do you compliment your partner on how cute/attractive/well-dressed/sexy they look? No matter how long you have been together, affirming you are still attracted to your partner is an important part of keeping the romance alive.

Be aware, too, how often you accept the positive messages sent to you by your partner. It is not only your responsibility to give and create positive moments, it is also your responsibility to be open to the positivity your partner brings to those moments. So if they give you a compliment, even if you don't think you are worthy of it or you question if they are being genuine, practise saying 'thank you'. It will help encourage your partner to be positive and may even draw you even a tiny step closer to each other.

When you are feeling distant, it is often difficult to be positive. Below is a couples' exercise to help the two of you reconnect with your own positive feelings about your relationship and your partner in a safe manner. This exercise is not a one-time fix: I would encourage you to repeat it weekly if you are experiencing a lot of problems and suspend talking about the problems until you both can recapture some of the positivity you have lost.

- *Step 1.* Take twenty minutes to remind yourself of as many positive moments/memories of your time together as you can – perhaps even write them down. Go all the way back to the beginning of your relationship and give yourself permission to focus on any interactions where you remember smiling and laughing together, being giddy and passionate together, being supportive of each other, listening to each other patiently, sharing joy and excitement and adventures together. Let yourself see the pictures of the two of you together; let yourself hear the tone of your voices; let yourself observe your partner's body language in those moments as you notice your own. Notice any distinctive smells that remind you of these good times and remember the feelings/physiological responses of your body as they touched you and shared with you.

- *Step 2.* Notice your own physiology (your heart rate, your breathing rate and depth) as you write down and remember these positive moments. It can be very helpful if you associate this moment with some physical gesture on your part. For example, you might at this moment of remembering put your right hand on your heart or perhaps cup your face with both of your hands. The gesture is up to you, to create and to remember. As you consciously breathe slowly and deeply, practise this gesture and say to yourself, 'When I put my hand(s) here, I remind myself of my love and admiration for my partner'. By recapturing the physiology of your romantic/warm/engaged feelings towards your partner, you can again recreate those feelings and experiences with your partner, even if there is distance now.

- *Step 3.* While practising this gesture, think about today with your partner and focus for now only on what qualities today you treasure about your partner. Be aware of your physiology, breathe deeply and slowly, and resolve to yourself, 'Today I am going to create a positive moment with my partner. Today I am going to talk with my partner about these warm memories and let them know I am committed to re-building, re-capturing and re-creating many more warm positive moments'.

- *Step 4.* It is now time to share with your partner. Ask them for ten minutes of their time and attention without any distractions. Tell them you want to give them a gift of positive memories of your time together. If possible, ask if you might touch them in some way that is comfortable for both of you as you deliver your gift. The touch may be holding hands or touching fingers. If possible, it might be helpful if you could re-create your gesture on your partner's body, to help ground you and connect you with those positive moments you remembered, and to help comfort and nurture your partner in the process.

- *Step 5.* After you have shared your positive memories and your intention to re-connect, allow yourself to listen. Really listen, and promise yourself, 'I will listen non-defensively; I will breathe slowly and deeply if I feel myself becoming defensive'. Remind yourself that the step you have taken today may need to be repeated many times in the weeks and months to come. Empathise with any difficulty they may have in hearing your words ('I know this may be hard for you to hear, believe or trust') while also asking them to be as open as possible ('I accept it may be difficult for you, and I ask you to be willing as much as you can to hear my words and know that I am saying them because I want to be closer to you'). Thank your partner for being willing to listen and for any touch that they have allowed.

Now switch roles and repeat all five steps.

If you are having chronic problems with communication in your relationship then you may need to contact a trained relationship counsellor. In the interim try a few of the tips in this chapter. Remember that if you can control how you communicate you are half way to solving the problem. In the next chapter on conflict you will learn more about why communication breaks down and how best to avoid repetitive, destructive behaviour.

HOW TO STOP FIGHTING

CHAPTER 3

To keep your marriage brimming
With love in the loving cup
Whenever you're wrong admit it;
Whenever you're right shut up.

OGDEN NASH

Time and again couples arrive at my clinic worn out and distraught from constant conflict, bickering, antagonism and disharmony in their relationship. When asked what they want from counselling, many simply respond that if they could stop fighting that would be a start! The irony is that I know of no marriage that is free of conflict. In my experience every couple is made up of two distinctly different people, with different experiences, interests and emotional predispositions. Regardless of the compatibility a couple creates in marriage, a husband and wife will always have somewhat different perspectives, and those differences will create conflict. Conflicts over money, careers, in-laws, sex, child rearing and a host of other issues are part of the experience of being married. By trying a few of the basic strategies outlined in this chapter, you can learn to deal with differences, hurt feelings and other common problems that often lead to fights. The first main ingredient for taking a new approach to old problems is agreeing to do so and agreeing on how to do so. If you are in a relationship with a person you love and you are not ready to throw in the towel and you want to try something different, this advice is meant for you. If you are involved in an abusive relationship or have simply had enough you probably need more than some basic advice.

Conflict is Important

To begin we need to accept that conflict cannot and should not be avoided. The number one predictor of separation and divorce is the habitual avoidance of conflict. What's sad is that the reason we avoid conflict is because we believe it will cause divorce. Conflicts can be productive, creating deeper understanding, closeness and respect, or they can be destructive, causing resentment, hostility and divorce. We need to realise that every happy, successful couple has approximately ten areas of disagreement that they will never resolve, some simple examples being individual taste in literature, music, food or type of car we like to drive. Very often couples will have differing opinions on what is good and bad in this area. There is a conflict of opinion but it does not necessarily need to lead to all out war! The real test is not how many conflicts occur, but how they are handled. Conflicts run all the way from minor unimportant differences to critical fights. There are conflicts of needs, wants, preferences, interests, opinions, beliefs and values. In this chapter we will describe simple steps to deal with conflict and ensure your relationship stays healthy, mutually satisfying and intimate.

In the beginning, couples avoid conflict because they are so much in love and believe that 'being in love' is about agreeing. They are afraid that if they disagree – or fight – they will ruin their relationship. Later, they avoid conflict because when they try to deal with differences things get so out of hand and fights become so destructive and upsetting that they simply shut down. After a few bad blow-ups, they become determined to avoid conflict at any cost. Successful couples are those who know how to discuss their differences in ways that actually strengthen their relationship and improve intimacy. These couples do not let their disagreements contaminate the rest of the relationship. While it is true that we don't get married to handle conflict, if a couple doesn't know how – or learn how – to fight or disagree successfully, they will not be able to do all the other things they got married to do. Or, put another way, it is hard to love each other if you are not speaking.

Unfortunately for many couples when it comes to resolving arguments, intuition prevails. Instead of resolving marital conflicts by creating and implementing a well-conceived plan, they revert to primitive instincts – demands, disrespect and anger. This may be due to how they learned to handle conflict in their family of origin or simply because they are not aware that how they deal with conflict is ineffective. These patterns not only fail to provide long-term solutions, but they also destroy the feeling of love. Because couples don't know any better, they keep using demands, disrespect and anger to try to resolve their marital conflicts until their love for each other turns into hate or indifference. We need to expose the assumption that we can repeat the same patterns of behaviour time and again and yet somehow expect a different result. Couples who have high levels of destructive conflict need to learn to distrust these primitive instincts and emotions. Many experts advocate that couples should be guided by their instincts whenever they have a conflict. Many falsely believe that the venting of these emotions can only be good: 'You can't beat a good row!'; 'It's the best way to clear the air.' Let's knock that myth on the head once and for all: fights, strong toxic emotions, anger, bitterness, sadness, bullying and abuse are not good for you, your partner or your children – they are bad for you and your family.

Styles of Conflict Resolution

The second principle in ensuring resolution of conflict is to understand that each individual has their own particular style of dealing with conflict. If you understand both your own and your partner's style you will save yourself a lot of grief and pain. This can be a hard thing to do as most people believe that it is their partner's obstinate behaviour that is the root of all arguments. This assumption is very, very wrong. Each individual needs to understand and accept that they are at least 50 per cent responsible. This is actually good news, as it means that you have within your control 50 per cent of the solution. John Gottman (1994) describes three styles by which individuals and couples resolve conflict and solve problems in their marriage:

1. **Validating**. This style involves frequent compromise and calmly working out problems in a fashion that benefits everybody.

2. **Volatile**. This style involves conflict erupting often, resulting in passionate disputes.
3. **Conflict avoiding**. This style involves agreeing to disagree; differences are rarely confronted head-on.

Recent research involving over three thousand couples (McKeown, 2002) indicates that about half of all men – both in their own assessment and in the assessment of their partners – tend to avoid conflict. However, although nearly 60 per cent of women see themselves as having a validating style, only four out of ten men experience them as such. Similarly, although about two in ten women see themselves as volatile, nearly twice as many men (38 per cent) experience them as volatile. Leaving aside the issues about which of these couples are in conflict, the research suggests considerable scope for differences in the manner in which each partner perceives, and is perceived by, the other. In other words, around 40 per cent of men and women see themselves quite differently from the way their partner sees them – at least in terms of how they resolve conflicts.

Often people assume that the gold standard in terms of marriage is for both partners to have a validating style and that volatile and conflict-avoiding marriages may be destructive. The fact is that all three styles are equally stable and bode equally well for the marriage's future. The key thing is for couples to be aware of their style and to manage their relationship accordingly.

Volatile couples use a wide variety of expression to influence one another. Positive affect (humour, affection, interest, teasing) as well as negative affect (disagreement) are maintained at high levels to create the image of passionate, persuasive, caring partners. Men who prefer volatile marriages are as likely to bring up tough issues as are women who are characteristically the issue bearers. These men also do not prefer to use stonewalling to cope with marital conflict, as is often the complaint of many wives of the other types. These volatile couples stay romantic for years. When deeper hurts are experienced they often renew their courtship. High value is placed on openness and honesty and movement to mutual independence.

Validating couples have their highest emotional energy use in the middle third of their interactions. Lower levels of emotion are expressed in the first or agenda building phase and the last or negotiating phase. The middle third is where the arguing happens and the couple finds that emotionally charged affect is best placed here and typically in moderation. These couples place their emphasis on 'we-ness' and companionship. Only central issues of importance are brought to the fore with emphasis placed on right timing. These couples are often characterised as 'friends or pals'.

Conflict avoiders will place their emotional expressiveness in the container of shared beliefs. They 'agree to disagree' and pursue more indirect discussions on hot topics. They moderate their highly charged negativity by minimising the importance of the problem, they gossip, talk of their mutual strengths and reconfirm mutual beliefs and commitment to each other. They end their conversations with solidity and optimism. This couple has been found more willing to explore their emotions and perceptions because their goal is acceptance and agreeing to disagree, not compromising, persuasion or problem solving. This style is often misrepresented as lacking psychological insight but they are the most validating and empathetically charged of all three types. They can take the risk to understand the interior of their partner's issues because their goal is acceptance. A conflict-avoiding husband presents this view, 'I'm reluctant to argue. It strikes me as wrong to expose disagreement or to seek it. The whole point is convergence'.

Recognise and Avoid Demand–Withdrawal Pattern

Couples in distressed relationships engage in a range of negative behaviours – particularly criticism, insulting, not listening and using force – which add considerably to their distress and further damage the relationship. The majority of troubled relationships involve couples who do not want to hear what their partner has to say. These behaviours are disastrous ways of interacting from the perspective of marital satisfaction. The experience of criticism from one's partner has a particularly strong effect on men while not being listened to by one's partner is the most negative influence on women's experience of the relationship. Both of these variables combine to illustrate the pattern of 'demand–withdrawal'. This is an established feature of distressed relationships between men and women where 'demand' is experienced as criticism and attack while 'withdrawal' is experienced as avoidance and denial; in this, as in all intimate relationships, the boundary between the real and the imagined is blurred. It is not difficult to see that this pattern may also be at the root of much of the mutual insulting which occurs between these couples and which has a somewhat more negative impact on women's sense of the relationship. This pattern is found time and again in troubled relationships whereby women's demands for change in a relationship are met by their partner's withdrawal in the face of those demands, possibly because her 'demands' are experienced as threats rather than invitations and his 'withdrawal' is experienced as a denial rather than as a difficulty. Generally when a woman is unhappy, she lets her partner know. She feels better afterwards because she has got it off her chest. It doesn't interfere with her love. She's trying to improve the relationship: 'If I tell him what makes me unhappy, then he will know how to please me; I am giving him a gift by telling him.' Unfortunately, many men don't see it as a gift. They feel criticised and put down. Instead of thinking, 'She feels lonely; I will move towards her and make her feel secure', they think, 'What is wrong with her? Didn't I just do that?' They pull away. If they come in contact with somebody else who says to them, 'Oh, you're wonderful!', then they may move towards that person. They may not be engaged enough in the marriage to work things out. The partner keeps trying and becomes more unpleasant because he is not responding.

Very often individual partners become too invested in getting their own way, or making extreme demands, and therefore are not being flexible enough to be fair with their partner. People often forget that there are usually several ways of doing things and that their own reality is not the only reality. We humans have a consistent tendency to believe that we are right and are being reasonable. In life in general, and in marriage in particular, you will be much more effective if you are willing to see the other person's view. So the next time you are in conflict with your spouse try to reflect on what is going on. Instead of getting stuck into repetitive behaviours try to understand that your reality is different to your spouse's. Step back and mistrust your gut; instead try some of the exercises below.

Mismatches and the Demand–Withdraw Pattern

There are a number of particular situations where couples have to be especially careful not to fall into the demand–withdrawal trap. The table below outlines some of these cases and the behaviour that occurs:

Validator with Avoider	The validator is constantly pursuing the avoider and feeling shut out emotionally. The avoider starts feeling flooded.
Validator with Volatile	The validator starts feeling not listened to and flooded, like they are doing combat duty all the time. The volatile feels that the validator is cold and unemotional, distant and disengaged. There seems to be no passion in the marriage.
Avoider with Volatile	This is the worst of the demand–withdrawal combinations. The avoider quickly feels that they have married an out-of-control crazy person. The volatile believes that they have married a 'cold fish' and feels unloved, rejected and unappreciated.

This table illustrates the perpetual problems that evolve from couples who are unaware of their conflict style. This lack of insight and therefore lack of ability to change can be the royal road to divorce. However, couples who stay together long term find a perfected expertness in their management of each other. These couples learn by trial and error to use positive affect (humour, affection, interest) to de-escalate conflict by communicating appreciation, softening the complaint and being non-defensive. They practice psychological soothing of self and other. It seems that the problems generated by their conflict style are less debilitating once both gain an awareness of their own and their partner's style. Happy couples seem to work at this together and slowly move towards problem solving or trying to make the unresolved issue a little bit better.

Breaking the Conflict Cycle

Consider your role in adding to the conflict. What can you do to break the conflict cycle? What do you often do wrong? How can you work together to resolve conflict more effectively? How can you repair damage that has been done?

When both of you are feeling relaxed, close and open, discuss the way you argue and what you could do to improve the situation. Think about the styles of conflict resolution and see which applies to you. Very often if a couple understands their conflict style they can avoid falling into the same trap time and again. The conflict avoidance process is a way of bringing clarity to what is very often a confusing, repetitive situation.

Conflict Avoidance Project

At a time when you are both refreshed and communicating well, review an argument you have had. Talk about what went wrong and how you could have found a solution more productively. Write down five guidelines for how you will next discuss a problem.

Each spouse should try to reflect on what is the spark or catalyst which leads to the behaviour kicking in. Is there a certain word or phrase which when used by their spouse causes an automatic anger reaction? Think about the whole area of demand–withdrawal. Is there anything you said or did that could have been perceived as a demand? Alternatively could your behaviour have been perceived as avoidant?

Spend some time alone reflecting on your differences. Come together and compare your lists. Be prepared to discover some surprises. Talk together about the times you feel your partner puts 100 per cent into your marriage. Share what you appreciate about your spouse; thank them for their contribution.

Heads over Hearts

As a cognitive therapist of many years' experience I have found the following formula to be the best way that couples can avoid the conflict trap. The first step is to understand that it is emotions that drive conflict. Think about it! People do not get into conflict over things about which they do not care. You are in conflict because something you care about is being undermined, ignored or getting out of control. The basic tenant of cognitive work is that it is not external events that cause emotions; it is your thoughts and cognitions, your mind.

The Brief Breather Process

The Brief Breather Process is a simple method for stopping the repetitive toxic fights that can leave couples hurt, powerless and without hope. It allows you to stop the cycle of insults and criticisms so you don't cause harm, and it allows time for cooling down until you are both thinking straight again and reconnecting from a better place.

The best way to learn how the Brief Breather Process works is to read through this section (when you're calm) so you will understand how it works when you really need it. Once you understand the four steps, practise using them whenever little things come up between you and your partner. Like all skills, this requires practice when not under pressure. You need to understand the theory and then try it out in daily life. That way, you will know the steps by heart when you are really under pressure and every bone in your body is telling you to defend and fight. This process is a shared concern: whilst you can learn and use it yourself, the real benefit occurs when both spouses learn and adapt. The process involves reciprocity and understanding. It is not a typical time out

– where one person banishes or abandons another; it is not about one person being put into the doghouse to get their act together. Instead with the Brief Breather Process, a time out begins with two people agreeing to separate in order to come back together after both have done some work on themselves. It is more than a cooling-off period. It is a Personal Reflective Space (PRS): a time to allow the brain to re-engage, to think about how our own thoughts and behaviours may be leading to communication problems, and to think about how we can help our partner – not fix them or bring them to our point of view, but instead listen and take on board their wishes.

This is where the healing begins. During a PRS, both people are expected to reflect on their own behaviour and are asked to take responsibility for having done things that may have hurt someone else. They are also asked to think how they could have made things better. The last step requires both people to make a peace offering, a gesture that restores a spirit of goodwill to the relationship.

Here are the four steps:

Step 1 – Take a breather!
As soon as you notice yourself getting uncomfortable with the way your conversation is going, PAUSE! Then say, 'I need some time in my personal reflective space'. This gives you a chance to take a break without blaming your partner for your discomfort.

Step 2 – Personal reflective space
This means physically separating from each other to stop the hurt escalating. It means going away for thirty to sixty minutes and returning when both of you have calmed down and have completed Step 3. It is important at this stage to realise that this is very different to withdrawing and avoiding. This is a planned approach, which, at its roots, is about caring for each other by avoiding the harm of toxic conflict.

Brain researchers have found that once the heart is beating 95 bpm or above, the thinking brain shuts down and the emotional brain takes over. This means it does no good to keep arguing when you are both upset because the reasonable part of your brain is no longer listening. Research on marital satisfaction found that couples who disengage when things start heating up and try again after both people are calmer, stay together and report greater satisfaction in their relationships. A simple test of this is to try to remember all the arguments you have had in the last year. I am sure you remember the hurt and intense feelings but very few people can actually remember what the argument was about. Put another way, once your body and brain go into fight or flight mode, love, compassion and all skills of communication go out the window. So stop wasting your time and learn how to interrupt this process. In many contact sports the real top athletes have learned to do this. The All Blacks rugby team have a concept called TEACUP. This means that each player has to learn to:

Think
Effectively
And
Clearly
Under
Pressure

This takes years to master. The core point in our context is that the personal reflective space is a tool to allow this to happen and to avoid using gut reactions and false perceptions that lead to isolation and disintegration of the relationship.

Step 3 – Own your part

This means taking responsibility for your part in creating the problem instead of attacking your partner or defending your position. Very often we revert back to infantile positions when trying to resolve conflict. The most common action being the 'blame game'. Remember your childhood, 'It wasn't me'? We also need to consider whether this is a genuine clash of unacknowledged worldviews. I often wonder at what stage couples realise they have moved from love to hate and finally to indifference. It is as if the couple have entered a war zone where one partner reflects a superpower with lots of resources and in-your-face tactics. In the face of this the other partner takes on the role of 'sniper in the ditch' or guerrilla tactics. To identify which role you may accidentally have taken on, answer the following questions:

Q: Have I engaged in any superpower acts of blatant bullying?
- Demanding obedience
- Controlling resources: money, freedom, time
- Using violence or threats to control my spouse
- Showing anger and contempt for my partner in public (includes attacks on character or appearance as well as acting as if my partner is invisible)
- Shouting or intimidating with words or gestures (includes sarcasm, mocking, finger-pointing, cornering, taunting)
- Blaming, belittling, interrogating, name-calling
- Hammering a point to death
- Ganging up on my spouse by bringing in kids, in-laws, other allies
- Excusing my bad behaviour by blaming my partner for it – 'I wouldn't drink if you weren't so controlling'
- Doing any of the above in front of our children.

Every act of blatant bullying by one partner can lead to just as many acts of equally powerful hidden mutiny by the other! Don't mistake submission for devotion, or obedience for love.

Q: Have I engaged in any guerrilla acts of hidden mutiny?
- Withdrawing or avoiding
- The silent treatment, refusing to talk
- Withholding positive feelings including affection, attention, tenderness, appreciation, sex
- Making excuses for why I didn't follow-through … again
- Making and breaking promises and agreements
- Procrastinating
- Constantly forgetting events or tasks

- Arriving home late
- Chronic apologies without subsequent changes in behaviour
- Flaunting my affection for others in front of my partner
- Lying or hiding the truth
- Bad-mouthing my partner to our children, friends, family
- Developing a social network that excludes my partner.

Q: What could I have done that would have been more understanding of my spouse, remembering that reciprocation and appreciation are the keys to success? Could I have been more helpful, more considerate, more kind?

Q: What worldview, thoughts or vulnerable feelings were beneath my anger or defensiveness? Do these feelings come from my family of origin?

Q: What vulnerable feelings might have been beneath my partner's behaviour? Am I sensitive to this and doing all I can to help them overcome these thoughts?

After you have answered these questions and have a better understanding of what went wrong and what part you played, you are ready for the last step: the unity gift.

Step 4 – Unity gift
Assuming you have done all three previous steps, you should be ready to come back together and talk. In turn, each partner should share what they learned about themselves in the reflective space. This means owning your part, apologising to your partner for the hurt you may have caused and offering a unity gift. A unity gift can be as simple as a hug or a kiss, or it can be a promise or an agreement to do something different. It can be the use of a name that indicates affection or a tender touch on the arm to reassure your spouse that you love them. When both of you have completed this step, chances are you'll be feeling lots better.

Here's an example of how this step might sound:

> I got angry because I wrongly thought that what you did was an attempt to make me mad. However, when I went through the lists and saw blaming, forgetting and excusing, I realised that I played a big part in what went wrong. I think I was annoyed and horrible to you because I was feeling guilty myself for forgetting to do X. Sorry. I know I hurt you. Next time I can try to be more honest sooner or I can at least stop blaming you before you have even had a chance to talk. I promise to do X by the weekend.

Like all skills this process requires practise. Practice taking a breather over and over until the steps are automatic. It takes lots of repetition, so hang in there! When you've perfected it, try teaching it to your kids. If they are too young to understand it, use the strategy in front of them. They will learn by example how to communicate lovingly and respectfully. Remember that you do not need to be in conflict to go into a personal reflective space: it can happen on the bus to work, on a coffee break or during a walk in the park. One thing is guaranteed: you will learn about yourself and, when the bad times hit, you will be in a better position to think effectively and clearly under pressure.

Stop Blaming
When couples are in conflict the marital relationship can often turn into a tug of war for power and control. When one member of the relationship is more dominant or doesn't permit the expression of the self or the other, the relationship will experience a halt in emotional growth and the couple will begin to experience disappointment, fear and worry. Anger will become the predominant emotion. It will envelop the relationship, leaving the couple with a sense of utter despair and confusion. At this point, many couples think about leaving the relationship because they just cannot understand and work with its dynamics and they cannot tolerate their conflicted feelings. The impulse to run away is

paramount. However, the reality is you cannot run away from yourself. It is essential that you know what your part is in the relationship that makes it not work for you. When each partner faces their inner feelings and behaviour patterns and takes responsibility for their actions, leaving the blame behind, the couple has the opportunity to repair their relationship. Blaming is usually a sign that we have lost control. As stated previously, it is a psychological immature position. If you begin to blame your partner for a problem, stop and ask yourself, 'What is my part in creating and continuing the problem?' Use your energy to figure out your part rather than to accuse or criticise the other. Once you have figured out how you contribute to the problem, share your thoughts and feelings with your partner and make the behaviour changes.

Controlling Toxic Anger

To finish this section I want to address a specific emotion that time and again is both the root and consequence of conflict. If either but preferably both individuals can gain control over their anger, toxic conflict can be avoided. Not that all anger is bad. On the contrary, anger can be justifiable and may be necessary, for example outrage over social injustice. Let us be clear about consistent personalised anger towards our spouse: it broadcasts our own weakness. When we vent our anger, we are effectively shouting, 'I'm scared! I'm frustrated! I'm hurt!', which is another way of saying, 'I'm weak!'. After all, we are only as big as the things that make us angry. Our first experience of anger caused by frustration may have been at birth. The infant doesn't want to leave the comfort and security of its mother's womb; nevertheless, it is forcibly expelled into a bright, noisy and cold world. The infant's frustration is understandable. However, as adults we need to accept the world as it is. When we understand this, we can begin to deal fruitfully with problems in our marriage and family.

When others do not follow our wishes or seemingly disrespect us, we become angry because of fear. We are afraid that we no longer have control over these people. However, we were never intended to control others. Guide others by our example? Yes.

Control others by power? No. Our desire for control is not wrong; it is just misdirected. It is ourselves that we need to control. When we give up our wish to control others and our environment, we will find that we have little to be angry about. Our partners are people and, just like anybody else at times, they will say and do stupid things. They can hurt us and, when they do, the temptation is to get angry. Nobody is perfect; we all have faults. How can we get angry with people for behaving like people? However, despite the many good reasons for not getting angry, it is a difficult habit to quit. That is because it's often more comfortable to feel angry than to acknowledge the underlying fear, frustration or pain.

It is important to remember that the consequences of one's anger are often far worse than whatever caused it. As a simple example, in a heated moment you may blurt out something you later wish you had not said. But the harm is already done. You cannot take back the past. The moral? Don't get angry!

Tips on Anger Management
- 'Anger will never disappear so long as thoughts of resentment are cherished in the mind. Anger will disappear just as soon as thoughts of resentment are forgotten' (Buddha).
- 'The greatest remedy for anger is delay' (Seneca). Counting from fifty backwards not only provides a delay, but shifts brain activity from the emotional part to the analytical part of the brain, decreasing the intensity of the unwanted emotion.
- Study relaxation and meditation techniques to reduce stress. Remaining calm allows you to examine the options and seek solutions. Getting angry blocks clear thinking.
- No one can make you angry. Whether you become angry or not depends on how you choose to react to circumstances.
- If your anger causes you to become physically or verbally abusive to your partner on a regular basis, you should seek therapy.

Finally, we should not forget that a lot of relationship conflict is caused by the everyday work of living with another adult and trying to raise happy children. Besides finances, choices that couples make over childcare and housework create more disharmonies between couples than any other issue. Couples often think that marriages should be made or broken on loftier issues than who takes out the rubbish, who changes a nappy or whether they are earning enough money relative to their neighbours. However, it is often the daily grind of sorting out who does what and when that eventually steers many couples to divorce court. Couples mainly fight about inequity of doing those tasks, or perceived inequity. One of the greatest sources of tension between couples is the female's perception that she is the one who does it all, that she has made the biggest compromises and that having a family has meant change for her only. A snapshot of how today's busy couple share their duties reveals there is the ideal split and the real life split, far from close. The ideal split is one in which both partners, regardless of how equal the work is shared, perceive it to be shared fairly. These partners will be the most satisfied with their work arrangement and with their marriage. In real life, however, only about one-tenth of couples believe they share work evenly at home. There is a big gap between what is ideal and what happens in real life. About one-half of women truly resent how they share these responsibilities. To overcome this it is important that both spouses sit down and, using the skills from the communication chapter, identify the perception/reality gap in this contentious area. Most people are used to doing audits in their work. This is a skill that we can transfer into this situation. The couple needs to spend time listing the actual tasks involved in keeping a nice home and raising happy children. This list is then compared to each spouse's perception of what actually happens. This usually brings up the fact that the huge investment by the female spouse is very often underestimated. Once the problem has been identified, recognised and appreciated it becomes easier to solve.

NEW PARENTS
AND BABA-GAGA

CHAPTER 4

*Please affix your own oxygen
before attending to your children.*

One of the biggest challenges that couples face is becoming parents. It is hard to believe that such a happy event, the entry of a beautiful new baby into the world, could actually be the catalyst for the slow decline into relationship conflict. How can a beautiful innocent baby lead to conflict, unhappiness and stress? In my work I have found that over 70 per cent of couples (McKeown, 2002) who seek help have children under the age of eleven. In this chapter we are going to look at the lessons learned from these couples. Each couple must learn to embrace the daunting roles of parenthood and absorb the impact of Her Majesty the Baby's dramatic entrance into the marriage whilst at the same time continuing the work of loving and living with their spouse. A simple way of saying this is that the focus needs to remain on a couple-centred marriage instead of becoming a child-centred marriage.

Each adult is initially born into the world as a son or daughter. We generally enjoy the bliss of childhood and the halcyon days of our youth. We live in a protected environment where when all comes to all we are able to fall back on the stability of our parents. We slowly move towards independence, developing our own personality and worldview. We reject some of our parents' opinions and supposedly outdated ideas, yet all the time we are living in a secure zone. In our teens and early adulthood we head out into the bright lights of encounter and with a bit of luck find a partner who we feel is gorgeous, intelligent and shoots electricity up our spine each time we see them. Even better is the revelation that this person feels the same about us! In their eyes we are a superhero or a goddess. Happy days! Love is in the air, it is real, the best ever feeling which can shield us from the slings and arrows of everyday life. In psychological terms, however, there has been no major movement. We are still psychologically working at the level of son and daughter. This psychological security helps us through this huge period of encounter. Eventually we decide that in the face of so much love we will get married. We set up home, take out a mortgage, buy a car, furnish the house, get promoted in work and generally enjoy the luxury of modern living. While all of these events are stressful in psychological terms we are still living as son or daughter.

Then one fine morning, whilst enjoying our existence and marital bliss, the biggest yet often most underrated psychological movement of our lives begins to happen. It may have been planned, hoped for and anticipated; alternatively it may catch us off guard. It can appear in the form of tiredness, a few extra pounds on the morning weigh in, a fluctuation in mood or a missed period. The suspicion grows and then, following a quick test, the truth unfolds. Yes, you've guessed it: you have moved in one instant from being somebody's son or daughter to becoming a mother or father. The psychological safety net is abruptly taken away. In a flash you need to get your head around the fact that you are becoming a mother or father. In your hands lies the safety and destiny of another human being! Nobody else will look out for this person like you. In your hurried busy life you now have to take stock and make room. It is a strange thing how nature can somehow be counter cultural. Surely mother nature should keep up with the times. Doesn't she know that time is money and speed is of the essence? Instead she sticks to the tried and trusted human pregnancy, which has no regard for comfort, couples and modern living. The strange thing about this psychological movement is that in key areas it is different for men and women. This beautiful secure couple now not only have to prepare for a baby but also have to go through a psychological change. Most couples are unaware of this change and so do not prepare for it; years later they wonder if this event was the beginning of the problems in their relationship.

Impending Parenthood

Let's address some of the issues that each of our budding parents faces. They will be newborn parents. Just like the baby, the two parents will be forced to enter a world that, very often, they have not been prepared for. So if you are the parents of infants or young children, take some time to reflect and think. Make sure you are providing a safe, secure and loving environment – not just for the baby, but also for your spouse and yourself!

In general, when a man is faced with impending fatherhood he will go to work. Please take this quite literally: the man will physically go to work. Men like action – when faced with something beyond their experience they will go into action. A new baby needs a lot of stuff – nappies, cots, clothes, a good school and a third-level education. The automatic thought in the man's brain is, 'Fathers must provide. Therefore I must get to work. In this way I will not have to think about this huge burden that is being placed on my shoulders'. Try to become aware of this automatic reaction: if you are a man try to avoid needless work; if you are a woman do not criticise your partner but gently remind him that his presence is something which makes you feel more secure and loved.

The woman, on the other hand, is struck by the here and now, the huge changes in her emotions and her body. A lot of things are happening that are beyond her control. One thing is for sure, however, and that is that safety and security are essential: 'Am I in a strong, loving relationship? Is this the basis for a strong, loving family? Am I alone?' In my experience one of the most consistent messages received from women in couple counselling is that it was during pregnancy that they began to feel alone and disconnected for the first time, typical comments being, 'John was so busy working' or 'He had just started a new job. I felt I was being too clingy'. On hearing of the impending baby, it is vital that you take your time, talk about your worries not just your anticipated joys and, most importantly, make sure as a couple that you make time for mother.

The human baby is one of the most vulnerable beings on the planet. Think about it: a young horse is on its feet in seconds; a young fish can swim; but a young human is born defenceless – semi-blind, lacking mobility. Parents must immediately provide food, warmth and security to ensure the survival of the new child. The immediacy of this need in the infant brings home to the new parents the sneaking suspicion that there is nowhere to hide: they alone are responsible for this young baby. Many couples report that on the drive home from the hospital it is still sinking in that they cannot give the baby back; that prepared or not their lives are about to change beyond all comprehension.

I want to try to bring you into the psychological world of the new mother. They have just been through nine months of physical change, gone into energy-sapping labour and have now been handed the responsibility of a defenceless infant. A striking perceptual shift occurs in the psychological makeup of the new mother. Put simply,

THE WORLD BECOMES
A MORE DANGEROUS PLACE!

By becoming aware of this shift couples can save themselves a huge amount of unnecessary stress. The ordinary, boring road the couple had used for years to commute to family or work can all of a sudden become a more dangerous place! The car that had sufficed up to now can easily be seen as a potential death trap! The corners of fireplaces, tables and counters now become hazards! The soothing peace of night-time slumber can become a time of worry for the new mother. Is the house safe? Is the room warm? Is the baby cold? This may seem like an exaggeration but it is all based on reports from new parents who were still adjusting to moving from the psychological safety of 'childhood' to the new demands of parental life.

Baba-Gaga

At this point I want to introduce you to the concept of 'baba-gaga'. This is a phrase that best describes the pressures faced by new parents, which, if not recognised and eliminated, can take over and ruin a marriage. At the start of this chapter, we referred to the importance of maintaining a couple-centred, rather than a child-centred, marriage. However, this can be difficult. Life before baby can seem like a distant memory; the couple, consumed with their new roles, can forget about each other. As stated earlier the first step to bringing balance back into your relationship with your spouse is to recognise the problem. If you found or are finding that your relationship has become 'baba-gaga' then the steps outlined below will help get you and your spouse back on track:

- Remember that you have two roles: you are both a mother and a wife or a father and a husband. You must make a pact that you will not stop being friends and lovers just because you are mums and dads.
- You need to renegotiate your relationship. Make a plan. Set a division of labour and time, and make a commitment to having fun and recreation in your life. Write it down and hold yourself and your partner accountable.
- Your plan should not be based on willpower, because willpower cannot carry you for the long haul. You need to reprogram your life and stick to it, so that when the emotion isn't there, the programming carries you.
- You must take care of yourself and each other if you want to take the best care of your child. You are your child's role models, so show them a good relationship.
- You need to be a couple and integrate your child into your relationship. You were a couple before your child, and you will be together when they become independent.
- Do not fight in front of your child – even a baby. It's just wrong and it is not the environment you want for your child.
- Remember the formula for a successful relationship: the quality of a relationship is dependent on the strength of its foundation and whether it meets the needs of the two people involved.

The best thing parents can do for their children is to keep their marriage strong. When the marital relationship is strong, couples tend to be better parents and children better adjusted. When 'baba-gaga' occurs most couples, in trying to figure out what is happening, don't want to blame the baby, but often attribute much of what has happened in their marriage and the stress that they feel in their marriage to personal weakness in themselves or their partner. Some marriages are weak to begin with and having a baby won't make them stronger. Irritants that were present in a marriage before a child's birth often resurface afterwards. Many couples think having a baby will bind them together forever, but we know this isn't true. Many marriages are affected negatively because new parents are generally unprepared for and then fail to cope with the changes that come into their lives after the baby is born.

Not all marriages are challenged after the birth of a baby, but all marriages are changed in some fashion. If we take a look over the long term, two in five marriages really don't change that much after childbirth and one in five actually improves over time. And, of course, many good relationships are further enhanced and strengthened by the birth of a child. Also, there are many couples that find that it is largely a positive experience. Currently 96 per cent of expectant parents attend childbirth preparation classes where they learn the mechanics of breathing, relaxation and many of the more practical aspects of being parents.

However, the responsibility of being a parent does not start with birth or the need to care for the baby. It starts with men and women caring for each other and in preparing for the role that each will play as the spouse of a new parent and not just the parent of a newborn. This is a role that few of us consider. Yet, playing this role well will largely determine the course a marriage will take after a baby is born. Men and women must really think about their marriage. Do they truly love each other? Do they really want to have this baby? Do they have the qualities to be a good parent? Does their spouse? Recognise that parenthood is a journey that calls for dedicated focus and sacrifice for a minimum of two decades, if not for a lifetime. And, for all the joy it brings, there will be hardships and heartache, too.

Sex After Baby

Very often the arrival of a baby correlates with a decline in the sexual activity of a couple. The turning point centres on resuming sex after the birth of a child and the frequency of lovemaking after its birth. Most men and women want to know if it is natural for them to stop making love after a child is born, if at least for a short time. They often want to know why lovemaking changes. They want to be encouraged to know whether the frequency of lovemaking will return. More than anything they want to know if what's happening to them is normal and if they should be fighting about sex. The goal should be at this time to keep sexual problems from becoming marital problems. The first thing couples need to understand is that there are no norms for sexual functioning at this time. If we look at some studies done regarding the sexual relationship of new parents as far as resuming lovemaking, the ranges are wide – anywhere from 30 to 80 per cent of new parents have not actually resumed lovemaking even by the sixth month postpartum check-up. Overall, there is about a 40 per cent drop in sexual activity within the first year after a child is born. Around 70 per cent of new parents report a change in their sexual behaviours within that first year postpartum. However, the thing to remember is that not everyone else is having great sex all the time either!

In marriage couples really do need to make love. It is one of the behaviours that cement and bond a marriage. Unfortunately, sex falls under the use it or lose it category. Continuity does count and once couples stop making love or allow large gaps to pass between lovemaking it does get harder and harder to get the ball rolling again. Couples also find that great pauses in sexuality actually cause hormonal levels to shift. So couples feel less in the mood to make love and, of course, as those hormones shift, usually their marital well-being shifts as well. To get back on track couples should be realistic and remember that all marriages, even the very best ones, go through periods where lovemaking lapses. You should put your lovemaking relationship into perspective. It is just a part but not the whole of your marital union. Perhaps you could work on other areas of your marriage or other areas of intimacy during this time.

It is important to have a frank discussion about how you feel about sex as new parents. Talk about the frequency and what seems right. However, remember to speak about other areas of your relationship that affect your ability or desire to make love, for example if you feel you need help around the house but your partner does not offer this help. If you are wondering as a couple where the romance went, consider the things you did when your romance was strongest. If you are no longer doing those things, make an attempt to start doing them again. Consider what outside stresses could be affecting each of you, individually and together – perhaps work, finances or something outside the home. Consider, too, if you are being critical of each other or making accusations and demands that might be a turn-off in the bedroom.

We should not forget that many mothers feel very insecure about bodily changes after pregnancy and childbirth. Self-esteem might be very low. If as a mother you are not feeling as fit and healthy as you used to, think about developing a self-improvement plan including healthy eating habits, exercise and a new and interesting hobby other than the baby.

A man places a great deal of importance on his wife's appearance. It is important to him to feel physically attracted to her. Adjusting to a mother's body or a woman's body and her image as a mother is not always easy for new fathers. However, a man should reassure his wife that he loves her for who she is and not how she looks at this particular time.

More than once I have heard men say that, 'Mothers aren't sexy. They wear wash-n-wear clothes and are usually too busy or too tired to make love.' Many of us still wonder how we ever came to be in this world. Our own parents make love? No way! For all of us as parents, we have conscious and unconscious thoughts we bring into parenthood about the sexual behaviours we expect of our spouses after we become parents. This is based on what we observed of our parents in their own marriage growing up. If we saw our parents being physically affectionate, we associate such intimacy with marriage and parenting. However, if we never saw our parents kissing, or doubted that they were ever physically close or attracted to each other, it may be difficult for us as parents to integrate sexuality with parenthood. So, in this case, couples need to think about the image they want to portray. If they want their children to think of parenting and marriage as fun, they should incorporate kissing and affectionate exchanges so their children can see them. A lot of men don't feel it is worth practising these specific behaviours. It can take time but with a little patience the feelings will return.

Finally, keep in mind that approximately one-third of new parents suffer low self-esteem, depression or other negative feelings about themselves during the first year postpartum. It is not unusual that new parents will find additional stresses in their relationship. However, the quality of the marital relationship remains the most critical factor in how a couple adjusts after the birth of the baby, so take on board what we have elucidated in this chapter, look after your child and most importantly take care of yourself and your spouse.

INFIDELITY AND HOW TO MOVE ON

CHAPTER 5

There are few people who are not ashamed
of their love affairs when the infatuation is over.
FRANCOIS DE LA ROCHEFOUCAULD

I thought that we had a special relationship, and now you have contaminated it; it doesn't feel special any more because you shared something that was very precious to us with someone else.

Infidelity is one of the most deeply wounding encounters in marriage. Most of us have certain assumptions about our marriage: that we chose someone and they chose us; that we have the same values; and that we have both decided to have an exclusive relationship. Even though we may have some problems, we love each other and therefore we are safe. When we find out our partner has been unfaithful, everything we believe is totally shattered. The fact that infidelity is usually unexpected and not part of our assumption about how a relationship operates causes traumatic reactions.

The extramarital affair is a far more complex relationship than the media often portrays it. Unlike Hollywood's portrayal of affairs, real 'love triangles' involve a great deal of guilt, confusion, anxiety and pain. They are complex and involve feelings, emotions and thoughts that are often conflicting and hard to manage. Extramarital affairs are usually concealed from friends and family, and most people quickly find themselves isolated, alone and trapped in maze of secrecy and dishonesty. Ultimately, all members of the triangle are affected, for better or worse. Whether the marriage survives or the lovers form a new couple, everyone involved will have been dramatically and permanently affected by the experience.

It is important to understand that you do not have to have intercourse to have an affair. There can be an affair without any kinds of touching at all: for example, people have affairs on the internet. Three elements determine whether a relationship is an affair. The first is secrecy. Suppose two people meet for a drink every evening after work and they never tell their partners. Even though it might be in a public place, their partner is not going to be happy about it. It is going to feel like a betrayal and deception. Emotional intimacy is the second element. A typical example of this is when someone starts confiding things to another person that they are reluctant to confide to their partner and the emotional intimacy is greater in the friendship than in the marriage. One common pathway to affairs occurs when somebody starts confiding negative things about their marriage to a person of the opposite sex. In reality, what they are doing is signalling, 'I'm vulnerable. I may even be available'. The third element is sexual chemistry, which can occur even if two people don't touch. If a person says, 'I'm really attracted to you' or 'I had a dream about you last night but, of course, I'm married, so we won't do anything about it', that tremendously increases the sexual tension by creating forbidden fruit in the relationship.

Fantasy is the main ingredient at the beginning of an infidelity. In this initial imaginary stage there is passion and romance, but we are still in the initial stages of relationship formation – idealising the partner. This first stage can go on for years, as long as there is a secretive and forbidden aspect. This admiration and positive mirroring continues until the infidelity becomes a reality-based relationship, which is why so many affairs end after the person leaves the marriage. Several clients have told me they wish the affair had never happened; they wish they had worked on their marriage instead. Once they got into the affair, it was too compelling. However, once the affair had settled into a reality-based relationship, they believed it was too late to go back to the marriage; they had destroyed too much.

People give many reasons for engaging in affairs. Some of these include dissatisfaction with the marital relationship, emotional emptiness, need for sexual variety, inability to resist new sexual opportunity, anger at a partner, no longer being 'in love', alcohol or drug addiction, growing apart and desire to get a partner jealous ... to name just a few. There are predicting factors that indicate a person's vulnerability to having an affair. Social context is the first predictor. If you are in an occupational or social group where many people have affairs and there is a sexually permissive attitude, you are more likely to fall into the same trap. The second predictor is if you come from a family where there is a history of affairs – the most notorious example being the Kennedy's, where the men in the family unit had a certain perceived entitlement. Coming from a culture where the double standard is alive and well is the third predictor. Some Mediterranean and Latin cultures attribute a great deal of importance to female sexual purity. Particularly among the upper social classes, women's virginity before marriage is a cultural imperative, and women's sexual behaviour is an important marker of a family's honour. Very often married women are expected to remain completely monogamous while accepting their husband's extramarital sexual affairs. Indeed experiencing sexual pleasure and gratification, even in marriage, may be interpreted as a lack of purity and virtue in a woman. Remember Tony Soprano!

There are two major factors that open the door towards infidelity:

1. Factors that PUSH and PULL people into affairs (perceived problems/faults/shortcomings of individuals or relationships; excitement, curiosity; enhanced self-image; 'falling in love' etc.)
2. Factors that MAINTAIN people in affairs.

Push and Pull Factors

Couples can create a pattern in their marriage that is not enhancing and the partner, instead of dealing with the dissatisfaction and trying to work on the relationship, escapes it and goes someplace else. When women have affairs, it is more often a result of long-term marital dissatisfaction. When she withdraws, the marriage is usually much further down the road to dissolution, because she has very often given up. Her husband, unfortunately, may think things are so much better because she is no longer complaining. He may not recognise that she has detached and become emotionally available for an affair. The husband may first notice it when his partner becomes disinterested in sex – or after she has left! He may then try everything to keep her. The tragedy is that is often too little too late. One thing is for sure: the desire for a new sexual experience is very rarely the initial motive for looking outside the marriage, but rather comes after the breakdown of the emotional relationship. Only then, after there has been an eroding of the interpersonal relationship, including a loss of passion, lack of intimacy and loss of emotional and sexual satisfaction, does the dissatisfied partner become open to the possibility of a new lover to fulfil their needs. If the interpersonal relationship was satisfying for both partners, and passion was still an integral part of the relationship, the need to experience diversified or new sexual partners may not exist. Respondents to a large-scale American study clearly indicate that their diminished 'feelings' for their partner led them to become involved in the extramarital relationship. Specifically, many people reported feeling unappreciated, ignored, sexually frustrated and no longer desirable to their partners. They almost invariably said that they were no longer 'in love' with their partners and lacked the level of intimacy that they once had.

Maintaining Factors

Research has identified several factors that may be responsible for the maintenance of extramarital affairs that may not have been considered before. These factors may be responsible for the high level of arousal experienced by people involved in affairs, the obsessive pre-occupation that many individuals in affairs report experiencing, and the inability to end an affair even when confronted with negative or devastating personal and social consequences.

In almost all cases the married member of an affair stated they felt 'more alive', 'more sexually appealing' and 'more appreciated' by their lovers than by their spouses. The unfortunate thing is that the way a person is different in the affair, if incorporated into the marriage, would probably make their spouse ecstatic. However, they believe they are stuck; they don't know how to create that opportunity for change within the marriage. A woman who was sexually inhibited in marriage – perhaps she married young and had no prior partners – may find her sexuality in an affair, but her husband would probably be delighted to encounter that new self. In the stories told to me of what happens during affairs, people seem to take on a different persona, and one of the things they liked best about being in that relationship was the person they had become. The man who wasn't sensitive or expressive is now in a relationship where he is expressing his feelings and is supportive.

An unpleasant factor that can often maintain an affair is the reality that once an affair begins it is not easy to end. Clients continually cite that they felt trapped. A particular worry is that if the affair ends, the affair partner may decide to tell people.

Watch those Boundaries
Affairs are less about love and more about boundaries. Affairs can happen in good marriages. The major attraction in an affair is not the love partner but the positive mirroring of the self – 'The way I look when I see myself in the other person's eyes'.

It is possible for all married people to fall for and be attracted to somebody else, even if you have a good marriage. In this collegial world where both sexes work together, you have to conduct yourself by being aware of appropriate boundaries, by not creating opportunities, particularly at a time when you might be vulnerable. That means that if you travel with a workmate of the opposite sex, you never invite them for a drink in the room; if you just had a fight with your spouse, you don't discuss it with a person who could be a potential partner. You can have a friendship, but you have to be careful whom you share your deepest feelings with. Although in general women share their deep feelings with lots of people, particularly other women, men are usually most comfortable sharing their feelings in a love relationship. As a result, when a relationship becomes intimate and emotional, men tend to sexualise it.

A key point to remember is that, as in many aspects of couple relationships, there can be gender differences when it comes to affairs. Men usually feel more betrayed by their wives having sex with someone else; women usually feel more betrayed by their husbands being emotionally involved with someone else. What really tears men apart is visualising their partner being sexual with somebody else. Women certainly do not want their husbands having sex with somebody else, but if it is an impersonal one-night fling, they may be able to deal with that better than if their husband was involved in a long-term relationship sharing all kinds of loving ways with somebody else. There are a number of specific points that couples can bear in mind to ensure they create clear and healthy boundaries around their relationships:

- Nurture a rational, wilful decision that extramarital affairs are deeply destructive and never an option. No circumstance or need or rationalisation will ever make adultery right or appealing. The answer to the question of having an affair is not 'I don't think so' but 'Never'.
- Do not keep secrets. Infidelity is based upon dishonesty. Bring all secrets in your relationship, even the small ones, out into the light.
- Keep all sexual fantasies focused on your partner.
- Set limits in casual relationships. Do not share intimate details of one's marriage or air dirty washing to a stranger, at work or in your social group. Mention your mate positively, refrain from long eye contact and avoid intimate settings. Affairs often start with a casual acquaintance and develop from there.
- Do not permit an intimate friendship to grow without tight boundaries. Boundaries can include ensuring your spouse is included in activities, no secret phone calls or texts.
- Do not play therapist and take part in bonding sessions over personal woes with persons of the opposite sex.

- Pay attention to pricks of conscience. People are seldom blindsided by an affair, but very often tend to ignore warning signals. A once-off prevention can be worth a pound of cure.

Rebuilding the Marriage

Once an affair has occurred ongoing honesty is essential to both personal recovery and to rebuilding the marriage. Honesty is more than just *not lying*; it is *not withholding relevant information*.

Although traumatic, infidelity can be a defining watershed for many marriages. My experience is that people are more willing to work through affairs than they were in the past. There is not the same kind of bitter resolution that people may have had in the past, when women would stay with an unfaithful husband because they had no place else to go. Staying together was more out of weakness; the marriage did not improve. Now people are saying, 'I'm willing to work through this, but we have to solve whatever problems we have; we have to get something out of this; our marriage has to be even better than it was before'. No matter how bleak things might seem, it is possible to revitalise a marriage wounded by infidelity. It is not easy and there are no quick-fix, one-size-fits-all solutions. However, years of experience have taught me that there are definite patterns to what people in loving relationships do to bring their marriages back from the brink of disaster. Healing from infidelity involves teamwork; both spouses must be fully committed to the hard work of getting their marriage back on track.

When a person discovers they have been cheated on, a psychological movement similar to a grief reaction can occur. A profusion of feelings, issues and reactions must be worked through. Elizabeth Kubler-Ross and other psychological researchers have demonstrated that there are typical phases a person goes through when grieving. Grieving is a vital part of recovery for the marriage because multiple losses have been incurred by both marital partners.

The first reaction is usually shock and denial: 'Could this really be happening? How could the person I love and trust do this to me?' All the years of energy and expectations seem to be lost in this act of infidelity. Later stages include anger, intense and wildly fluctuating emotions and tears, depression, feeling duped, bargaining and interrogation, confrontation, and many flashbacks and fears. All stages and feelings have to be experienced and worked through before healing can begin and the infidelity resolved. By continually asking questions the aggrieved spouse is actually helping the relationship to recover. It helps to break through the shock and denial, and ensures anger is ventilated as opposed to buried. It allows the couple to elicit what was going on and thus prevent another affair from happening. It allows the partner to break the bonds and completely reclaim their spouse by destroying all secrets ensuring all knowledge in the relationship is mutually shared. The single best indicator of whether a relationship can survive infidelity is how much empathy the unfaithful partner shows for the pain they have caused when the betrayed spouse begins to question and repeat the story of the trauma they are suffering. This can lead to major emotional upheaval, which is painful for both partners.

The unfaithful spouse needs to work through this by:

- Answering all questions and hanging in through the inevitable emotional turmoil
- Severing contact with the third party and building trust through actions, not promises
- Making a commitment to honesty and ongoing honest communication
- Accepting the fact that monogamy is an issue that is never settled 'once and for all' but requires ongoing effort/ commitment.

The following tips may help the person who has been betrayed to recover from the emotional impact:

- Accepting the fact that it happened (no more 'if only …' or 'why me?')
- Deliberately focusing on dealing with it and talking openly about what happened

- Allowing time to heal and, most of all, believing it is possible to recover. Understanding that this is not just personal failure, that structural and societal factors as outlined earlier play a part as well. Looking at affairs only as a personal failure of you or your spouse or your particular marriage inevitably leads to personal blame, personal shame, wounded pride and almost universal feelings of devastation.

Although some people are more curious than others, it is very common to have lots of questions about the affair, especially initially. This is all part of the healing process. If you have little interest in the facts, so be it. However, if you need to know what happened, ask. Although the details may be uncomfortable to hear, just knowing your spouse is willing to 'come clean' might help you recover. As the unfaithful spouse, you might feel tremendous remorse and guilt; you might prefer to avoid the details entirely. However, experience shows that this is a formula for disaster. Sweeping negative feelings and lingering questions under the carpet makes genuine healing unlikely.

Once there is closure on what actually happened, there is typically a need to know why it happened. Betrayed spouses often believe that unless they get to the bottom of things, it could happen again. Unfortunately, since the reasons people stray can be quite complex, the whys are not always crystal clear. No one forces anyone to be unfaithful. Infidelity is a decision, even if doesn't feel that way. If you were unfaithful, it is important to examine why you allowed yourself to do something that could threaten your marriage. Were you satisfying a need to feel attractive? Are you having a 'mid-life crisis'? Did you grow up in a family where infidelity was a way of life? Do you have a sexual addiction?

It is equally important to explore whether your marriage is significantly lacking. Although no marriage is perfect, sometimes people feel so unhappy they look to others for a stronger emotional or physical connection. They complain of feeling taken for granted, unloved, resentful or ignored. Sometimes there is a lack of intimacy or sexuality in the marriage. If unhappiness with your spouse contributed to your decision to have an affair, you need to address your feelings openly and honestly so that together you can make some changes. If open communication is a problem, consider seeking help from a qualified marital therapist or taking a communication skill-building class. There are many available through professional organisations and private practitioners.

Another necessary ingredient for rebuilding a marriage involves the willingness of unfaithful spouses to demonstrate sincere regret and remorse. You cannot apologise often enough. You need to tell your spouse that you will never commit adultery again. Since you are working diligently to repair your relationship, you might think your intentions to be monogamous are obvious – they aren't! Tell your spouse of your plans to take your commitment to your marriage to heart. This will be particularly important during the early stages of recovery, when mistrust is rampant.

Conversely, talking about the affair cannot be the only thing you do. Couples who successfully rebuild their marriages recognise the importance of both talking about their difficulties and spending time together without discussing painful topics. They intentionally create opportunities to reconnect and nurture their friendship. They take walks, go out to eat or to a film, develop new mutual interests and so on. Betrayed spouses will be more interested in spending discussion-free time after the initial shock of the affair has dissipated.

Ultimately, the key to healing from infidelity involves forgiveness, which is frequently the last step in the healing process. The unfaithful spouse can do everything right, be forthcoming, express remorse, listen lovingly and act trustworthy and still the marriage will not mend unless the betrayed person forgives their spouse and the unfaithful spouse forgives themselves. Forgiveness opens the door to real intimacy and connection. But forgiveness doesn't just happen; it is a conscious decision to stop blaming, make peace and start tomorrow with a clean slate.

The following are some key tips to help avoid infidelity:

What Will Not Work
- Assuming it could never happen to you
- Being 'in love'
- Promising to be faithful
- Threats or ultimatums
- Religious commandments
- Having more children
- Repeating the marriage vows
- Spicing up your sex life
- Trying to be 'perfect' and trying to meet all your partner's needs.

What Is More Likely to Work
- Being aware that no one is immune from having an affair
- Making a commitment to honesty (rather than just a promise of monogamy)
- Engaging in ongoing honest communication about everything that impacts your relationship, including attractions to others
- When you feel the urge to enter into an affair, read this chapter, stop and think about what is going on in your marriage.

Healing from infidelity takes a long time. Just when you think things are looking up, something reminds you of the affair and you go downhill rapidly. It is easy to feel discouraged unless you both keep in mind that intense ups and downs are the norm but that, eventually, the setbacks will be fewer and further between.

INFORMATION TECHNOLOGY, OVERLOAD AND ADDICTIONS

*Technology is a way of organising the universe
so that man doesn't have to experience it.*

MOTHER TERESA

No matter where we look, technology is changing and shaping our lives. Twenty years ago computers, mobile phones and the modern information age did not exist. Now it is so pervasive that it warrants a chapter all to itself in this book. It is truly amazing to think that we actually used to live without mobile phones, blackberries and laptops. Whilst all of this has led to better connectivity and a greater ability to communicate, it has also created a context in which it can be hard to stop and give time to your marriage and family. If you don't believe me, walk to your local shopping centre and spend a while people watching. You may notice that a large number of people are not mentally present to the people they are physically with: the man having lunch, but at the same time texting a friend; the mother speaking on the phone, while trying to shop and watch a young child; the child busy playing a game on the phone, while his parents queue up for coffee. All these examples display how it is becoming harder for people and, in this instance, married couples, to set a context in which they can slow down and attend to each other. In this chapter we will examine some of the basic scenarios where technology can eat into the marital space. Then we will go on to the more pathological areas of internet affairs and addictions, which sadly are a growing phenomenon in the modern marriage.

A married person needs to have a trusted partner or spouse who is available to them. Married couples need time to talk and be together. Families need time together to love and be loved. Modern technology if not well-bounded can begin to eat into that caring space. To illustrate I want to provide a small snapshot of the healthy modern couple. No addictions, gambling or compulsive behaviour in terms of technology. Instead we are entering a normal family home in modern Ireland. Take the simple microwave, for example. This small, somewhat old invention can have an impact on quality time if not used properly. Most couples have a desire within themselves to sit down together for a family meal, to be there as man and wife in front of their children. Add in the microwave and all of a sudden it is easier for one parent and the kids to eat together. The other spouse can heat up theirs when they come home. This once off event can develop into a pattern and it has now enveloped the modern family. The simple microwave facilitates a breaking of some of the core rituals that help a family to bond. 'Why should I get the 5 p.m. train to get home in time for tea? I could just get the 6 p.m. train and zap my tea instead!' So we arrive in the door at 7 p.m., but just as we are putting down our laptop, the mobile rings. Whilst talking on the phone, we use the microwave to heat and eat. A quick check of our email while continuing our phone chat, all is well but need to finish as a match is on Sky sports at eight. Trip up stairs to change and see the wife and kids – alas they are all watching Dora on the TV in the main bedroom, best to leave them alone. Watch the match, go to bed, get up in the morning – and here we go again!

The above is a snapshot. If it represents your life then it is time for change. Make sure your life, your family and most of all your marriage are not being lost in the middle of new technology. Try to set up an environment where you are both physically and psychologically present to your family. Be selfish about this! Technology, specifically the internet, is adding an extra burden to families. If not contained it can lead to some serious problems in relationships. The trend towards this is growing at such an extent that I believe in a few years it will be one of the major reasons for marital break up cited throughout the divorce courts.

Do you Spend Too Much Time Online?

There are people who compulsively chat online, people who compulsively download pornography and people who compulsively play games and gamble on line. If the word 'addiction' is even appropriate, I would like to suggest that people become 'addicted' to these activities and indeed to the internet itself. The term 'internet addict' is not an official diagnostic term, though it is sometimes used to describe someone who is compulsively using the internet and seems to be addicted. Many of these people can appear to be high flyers and a product of the modern age. They understand the technology, may have all the gadgets and do not consider that they have a problem. We don't consider them to be addicted. But how can you tell if you are or not? For most addictions and compulsive behaviour, professionals use the following criteria to make a diagnosis (Griffiths, 1997):

- **Salience**: the activity becomes the most important activity in a person's life
- **Mood modification**: feeling a buzz or high, or feeling numb or tranquil
- **Tolerance**: increasing amounts of the activity are needed over time to produce the same euphoric effect
- **Withdrawal symptoms**: unpleasant feeling occurring when the activity is ceased
- **Conflict**: interpersonal conflict because of the activity and intrapersonal conflict within the individual
- **Relapse**: the tendency to repeatedly revert to earlier pathological patterns of use, and for the most extreme patterns of use to be quickly restored after many years of control or abstinence.

The major problem with internet addiction is that it is socially acceptable and not seen as a problem by society in general, except of course by the increasing numbers of couples who speak about their problems in counselling. The addicted person is not falling in the door drunk or causing a public spectacle. They are intelligent, hard-working people capable of giving genuine explanations and reasons for their behaviour.

In the general run of life, 'addictions' can be healthy, unhealthy or a mixture of both. If you are fascinated by a hobby, feel devoted to it, would like to spend as much time as possible pursuing it, this could be an outlet for learning, creativity and self-expression. Even in some unhealthy addictions you can find these positive features embedded within the problem. But in truly pathological addictions, the scale has tipped. The bad outweighs the good, resulting in serious disturbances in one's ability to function in the 'real' world. On a more practical level, problematic addiction can be defined as anything that never really satisfies your needs and which in the long run makes you unhappy – *that disrupts your life*. In this instance we are talking about your marriage and family life – the ability to spend quality time with your spouse and children and to actually be psychologically present. Here are some questions that may help to determine if your relationship with technology is interrupting and eating into your marriage:

- Are you neglecting important things in your life because of this behaviour?
- Is this behaviour disrupting your relationships with your spouse and family?
- Do your partner or children get annoyed or disappointed with you about this behaviour?
- Do you get defensive or irritable when your partner criticises this behaviour?
- Do you ever feel guilty or anxious about what you are doing? Have you ever found yourself being secretive about or trying to 'cover up' this behaviour?
- Have you ever tried to cut down but were unable to?
- If you were honest with yourself, do you feel there is another hidden need that drives this behaviour?

An affirmative reply to one or two of these responses may not indicate anything; an affirmative reply to many of them means trouble. It may be a variation of what psychologists are calling the Internet Addiction Disorder. It is important to remember that technology will only ever grow more websites and gadgets, and that chat rooms will develop over the next few years. Technology is here to stay. If you are already having problems, they will only get worse unless you address the issue.

The Internet and Information Technology

If we drill down a bit further we come across three particular problems that drive a couple apart. The first area where the internet and information technology is becoming a problem for relationships is how it facilitates infidelity. As we have noted for some people the computer itself is very addictive. They get very caught up in it. It is a cyber version of hiding out and escaping. The typical forum for this is the online chat room. Think back to what we learned about affairs and infidelity, how they can be an escape from the realities of everyday life. In the modern world these two escapes are now paired. When online, people can disguise who they are. Think of the roles you can take on if you hide behind a computer screen. At the computer, with a screen in front of you, you can act out any fantasy you want. You can be anyone you want to be. You can make this other person become anybody you want them to be, because the relationship begins in anonymity. There's a loosening up, because you are not face to face with the person. Many people say that on the net they feel they are *more* like their true selves than in real life. They are more open, expressive, warm, witty and friendly. Once again, partial anonymity (not being seen or heard in person) allows people to be less inhibited. In some ways it is not unlike the poet, writer or artist who through their work learn to fully express themselves without fully being in the presence of others. It is all in the realm of fantasy. The internet facilitates the quick slipping of the user into fantasy. If you are talking to somebody on the computer and you begin to talk about your sexual fantasies, and you are not talking to your partner about your sexual fantasies, which relationship now has more sexual chemistry? Which relationship has more emotional intimacy? Then your partner walks in the room and you switch screens. Now you've got a wall of secrecy. It has all the components of an affair and it happens very easily. If this sounds familiar to you, go back to the chapter on infidelity and take it on board.

Technology has impacted affairs in another way, too. Many people have discovered their partner's affair by getting the mobile phone bill, by taking their partner's phone to check who has been calling or discovering secret text messages. We are leaving a whole new electronic trail. In the past, when someone was suspicious they could ask their partner, 'Are you involved with somebody else?' or 'What's going on? You seem distant lately'. If the partner denied there was anything wrong, there wasn't a whole lot somebody could do. Now there is tangible evidence people can find to discover if their hunches are indeed justified. This whole reality creates and enhances a web of deceit, dishonesty and mistrust. In this atmosphere it is only a matter of time before love crumbles and the relationship ends.

Internet Pornography

The second major problem area facilitated by the internet is pornography. One of the spouses (usually the man) can develop an internet pornography habit. This habit is more than porn *per se*; it is also the rush of finding websites, getting backdoor passwords, scouring file-sharing sites. This usually gets recognised when the person is visiting these websites daily. It begins affecting work attendance and performance, as very often the habit involves staying up late and doing things secretly when their partner is unaware. In order to keep the habit secret the person usually begins to tell lies. Their obsession becomes narcissistic to the point where they can only gain sexual pleasure via the repetitive accessing and viewing of sites. This, of course, has an impact on the marital relationship because sexual energy is diverted from the spouse into the obsessional activity.

Clients often report scenarios in which partners spent a disproportional amount of their time, attention and energy on porn, and resorted to lying and deception to support their habit, which contributed greatly to the destruction of their relationship.

The problem isn't just the pornography; it is how the habit becomes so time-consuming, and how it is combined with so much secrecy and lying, causing feelings of hurt and rejection.

Internet Gambling

Very few people have any kind of understanding of the devastating impact that a gambling habit can have: it wrecks your marriage, alienates your family, leaves you in financial ruin – basically it takes over and destroys your life. Gambling starts as a bad habit, something that a person does when they have some spare time, but it quickly worms its way into their daily routine and becomes an all encompassing and hard to break addiction that rules their life. Like alcohol abuse, gambling is often a root cause for domestic violence and child abuse.

The potential problem has been made worse and gambling has become even more common because of internet gambling. It is one of those increasingly common marriage problems that is often overlooked, despite research indicating that over 50 per cent of compulsive gamblers are divorced. There are now around 1,700 gambling websites all vying for business, just waiting to encourage more and more people into the regular gambling routine. Online gambling is a really bad habit to get into with the 24/7 access from the comfort of your own home, the loss of the sense of reality when gambling away money and the ease with which the gamblers can add more funds. Research (Gregory, 2005) has shown that online gamblers are more likely to have the most serious gambling habits / addictions and the families of those addicted suffering a greater intrusion into their everyday lives.

Obsession has always been with us in various forms, from the harmless to the seriously weird, from the ditzy to the dark and downright dangerous. The melting pot of cyberspace makes no judgements. The gambling obsession on the internet is particularly vicious and effective as it is masked in the trappings of business, professionalism and good fun. All the online bookmakers and gambling syndications sponsor many of our national media and broadcasting forums. This is evidence of how acceptable their profit making at the sake of family life has become.

Gambling over the internet first became available to users of the World Wide Web back in the mid-1990s when the Caribbean islands began issuing licenses to individuals and companies to enable them to operate gaming websites of this type in a legal manner. The individuals who owned the online gambling websites would pay the Caribbean government to operate such sites. From that time to the present, online gambling websites have been widely utilised and it does not appear that they will lose popularity any time soon. With the introduction of gaming over the internet, gambling addicts were faced with a new hurdle to jump over. For these individuals, resisting the urge to gamble at their local bookies or arcade was hard enough but with this newly acquired access to gambling from the comfort of their own living room, a new type of monster reared its ugly head. Now their addiction would be harder to resist due to the sheer availability of online gaming websites.

With any addiction, convenience not only fuels the fire but is the main reason behind the crash and burn aspect of it all. It is very hard to resist something that is at the tip of your fingers, twenty-four hours a day, seven days a week.

You can sit in the comfort of your own home, go online and wager money on automated games such as blackjack, poker, roulette and more. The only things an individual needs so they can gamble online are a computer, internet access and a credit card. Once those items are obtained, that person can start playing games online for money. Because the person is not using hard cash they can very often build up big losses without realising it.

The aspect of knowing that if you play just one more game you might be able to win a lot of money is very tempting. This propels the individual to play more and more each day, thereby forming an addiction to online gambling.

Overcoming Online Gambling Addiction

Fortunately for individuals who are battling an online gambling addiction, there are people and organisations available to help.

Gamblers Anonymous focuses not only on gambling in a traditional sense but on online gambling problems as well. The basis of Gamblers Anonymous is to organise a place for individuals with gambling problems to meet anonymously and talk about the reasons behind their addiction and what can be done to help them through these hard times. If a group setting is not the type of arena in which you wish to discuss your gambling addiction, individual therapy is another form of treatment. Professionals in the mental health field will often hold individual sessions with those who have gambling problems and try to help them through this terrible addiction.

If any of the above problems apply to your relationship then you really need to get serious about tackling it. In many instances the spouse of the user can enable the behaviour by making excuses or saying that it is not a problem. This is understandable, but in the long run will not solve the problem. If you believe your partner has a problem you need to bring it out into the open using some of the communication techniques outlined earlier in this book. Above all you have to be careful not to collude or sign up to dishonest or avoidant practices. If you feel that the problem is too much for you to solve alone then seek help from some of the professional resources outlined at the end of the book.

The first thing a user has to recognise is that all of this activity lies in the realm of unhealthy fantasy. Deleting everything you have is a good start, as is getting rid of all the bookmarks and file-sharing services. The harder you make it to get at, the better chance you will have of resisting the temptation. As with cigarettes, the craving will pass after five to ten minutes. In time the cravings will become less frequent. 'Abreaction' is a simple but proven technique to interrupt addictive patterns. This involves a small painful stimulus being activated each time you feel like engaging in the destructive behaviour. Try the rubber band technique (keep rubber band against wrist, snap it whenever you think of pornography). Like any other mental addiction, you get a rush of exciting chemicals to the brain whenever you indulge the craving; this is what you are really addicted to. Learned behaviour can be unlearned, but there is no sure-fire cure for any addiction besides being forcibly deprived of getting at that which excites you. People are slaves to habits, either good or bad – it is inescapable human nature – so you might as well cultivate good habits and not destructive ones. You will need a new hobby, and it should be away from the computer. Maybe watch sports after work; go to a local gym that is open at night and have a quick workout and sauna; read a book you have been meaning to read but never found time. Better still, instead of staying up late to feed your habit, go straight to bed and cuddle with your wife until you unwind and fall asleep.

Try limiting the time you spend online too. What has helped with my clients' computer over use is to turn the computer off a lot, instead of always having it on and available. Develop a schedule where you check non-pornographic and non-gambling sites and your email at certain times, and then shut the computer off. Consider moving the computer to a more public area of your house. If your work demands a lot of computer work. Have another computer with no internet if you need to do work on offline things. Try to keep your time scheduled so that you are not faced with a lot of time home alone with the computer.

The fact that you are reading this book and particularly this chapter is an encouraging sign. It may seem like a huge step to gain control over an addiction, but remember it is from little changes that new behaviours grow. If you take one day at a time, you will find this task more manageable. Give yourself positive messages and acknowledge the progress you make. The human spirit within all of us provides an unlocked potential for change. If you take time to look within and listen to the messages of your heart then change will occur.

WORK–LIFE BALANCE

CHAPTER 7

We live in a moment of history where change
is so speeded up that we begin to see the present
only when it is already disappearing.

R.D. LAING

Are we living to work or working to live? This is a key question that arises for many married couples. Most agree that the preferred option is to work in order to provide a source of income and then have time to enjoy life. We all have to work and make a living. The money we earn is what in the real world supports our family. As Bill Clinton once said, 'Money is not everything, but it is up there with oxygen!' However, to maintain a strong and healthy relationship couples need to ensure a healthy work–life balance. One of the major problems stated by couples is that their work life and personal life tend to be somewhat out of balance. The challenge of achieving a work–life balance is central for all married couples.

Changes in family roles indicate that today's married couple are typically part of a dual-career household, which makes it difficult to find time to meet commitments to home, spouse, parents and friends. If you have experienced any of these challenges, you understand how easy it is for work to overtake your personal life.

Before couples can move forward they need to realise and figure out what work–life balance means to them. If couples can work this conundrum out, their future life together will be dramatically better for it. In the modern age of results-driven living most workers need to be obsessive, work incredibly hard and generally end up maxed out. This manifests itself in many ways, including always being overcommitted, regularly being exhausted and having a marriage and home life that is squeezed into leftover time. Career wise, the modern couple are very successful at the work they do. We live in the richest part of the world, with big houses, big cars and generally secure economic means. Many of my clients have created a company, achieved excellence in their work and become financially comfortable. However, this can come at a cost of low – or no – balance in life. Many married couples are on the road from Monday to Friday, arriving home exhausted at the end of the day. Weekends turn insidiously and unknowingly into 'recovery time' when most modern couples are playing catch up on all the tasks they could not get done during the week or else staying in bed trying to catch up on some sleep. The burnout cycle continues year on year, every six months completely crashing from the effort – drinking too much, struggling with weight and feeling physically below par.

The above paragraph describes the typical couple whose marriage is under pressure. If this resonates with your current situation, there is only one thought that can change this. You may have had the thought in the past, you may have it now, but make no mistake unless you take corrective action you will still have it in the future. This simple thought is this:

> I'm done. I'm not mad – I just can't do this anymore. I either have to change, or it's over.

The good news is that you have woken up! Well done and welcome to reality. Once you have discovered that you want balance the next step is to develop simple habits to achieve this goal.

When people spend more time at work than at home they miss out on a rewarding personal life. Furthermore, if they are trying to care for children or cope with marital, financial or legal problems, it becomes hard to concentrate on their job. One of the major reasons for this is that in the modern world we exist within blurred boundaries. This allows and in many cases actively encourages the job and career to creep into your personal time. In the 1960s and

1970s, employees showed up for work Monday through Friday and worked eight to nine hours. The boundaries between work and home were clear. Unfortunately, for many people, that is no longer true. Your work life may be spilling over into your personal life, blurring the line between your work and your family. There are a number of reasons for this. If you are aware of the reasons you are well armed to defend your family life, personal time and move towards your favoured position of working to live.

Globalisation of economics and business means that work continues around the world twenty-four hours a day. If you work in a global organisation, you might be on call twenty-four hours a day for troubleshooting or consulting. Improvements in communication technology mean that people now have the ability to work from anywhere – their home, their car – and even when they are on holidays. In the current profit-orientated culture it is not unusual for an employer to ask staff members to work longer hours than they are supposed to do. For some workers, overtime may even be mandatory. If you hope to move up the career ladder, you may find yourself working more than forty hours a week on a regular basis to keep on top of things or exceed expectations.

For many people it is tempting to work overtime. Many of us can remember the dark days when you were lucky to have an income, never mind earn extra. By doing so, you can earn money for that new car, your child's education or your family holiday. Some people, particularly those on hourly rates, need to work overtime to stay on top of family finances. For others, working extra hours may not bring extra cash, but it can help keep up with your workload. Being willing to arrive early and stay late every day may also help people climb the corporate ladder. If your company does not require overtime, take a few minutes to think it over before you agree to work more than a forty-hour week. Take a few deep breaths, count to ten and assess the pros and cons:

- **Fatigue.** Your ability to think decreases when you are tired. This means that by the time you get home you are ready for bed, as opposed to being ready to spend time with your family. Do not allow your cherished family time to pass you by.

- **Family**. You may miss out on important events, such as birthdays or your baby's first steps. Missing out on important milestones may harm relationships with your loved ones.
- **Friends**. Trusted friends are a key part of your support system. However, if you are spending time at work or in the office instead of with them, you will find it difficult to nurture those friendships.

If you work for a company that requires mandatory overtime, you will not be able to avoid it. In this situation, it is possible to plan around and limit it. If you work overtime for financial reasons or to climb the corporate ladder, do so in moderation. Most importantly, say no when you are too tired or when you have crucial family obligations. Examine your priorities and set boundaries. Be firm in what you can and cannot do. Only you can restore equilibrium to your lifestyle.

Finding the Best Balance

It isn't easy to juggle the demands of career and personal life. For most people, it is an ongoing challenge. Here are some options to help you find the balance that is best for you, your unique situation and most importantly your relationship.

- *Keep a log*
  Track everything you do for one week. Include work-related and non-work-related activities. After you see your patterns, decide where to make adjustments. Cut or delegate activities you don't enjoy, you don't have time for or you do only out of guilt.

- *Manage your time*
  Organise household tasks efficiently. Doing one or two loads of washing every day rather than saving it all up for your day off, and running errands in batches rather than going back and forth several times from your home are good places to begin. A weekly family calendar of important dates will help you avoid deadline panic. Find out if your employer offers a course in time management. If possible, sign up for it.

- *Rethink your cleaning standards*
  An unmade bed will not alter the course of your life. Do what needs to be done and let the rest go. If you can afford it, pay someone else to clean your house.

- *Communicate clearly*
  Eliminate time-consuming misunderstandings by communicating clearly and listening carefully. Take notes if it helps. Try to avoid taking phone calls in your own time. Instead insist that the problem will be discussed and solved when you are back on work time.

- *Nurture yourself*
  You cannot have a job, family and friends without nurturing yourself. Try to set aside some time each day for an activity you enjoy, such as reading, or listening to music. Decompress after a hectic workday by taking a walk, going to the gym or taking a bath or shower. You and your family can decompress by spending the first fifteen minutes at home at the end of the workday together without having to concentrate on a household or work task.

- *Set aside one night each week for recreation*
  Take the phone off the hook, power down the computer and turn off the TV. Discover activities you can do with your friends, partner or family, such as making a favourite family dinner together, playing a game or going for a walk as a family. Making time for activities you enjoy will rejuvenate you and connect you with your spouse and family.

- *Protect your day off*
  Try to schedule some of your routine household chores on workdays so that your days off are more relaxing. Try to keep at least one day a week free from washing, ironing and work. Instead devote it to family activities. Guard this time from all predators who might try to eat into it.

- *Get enough sleep*
  There is nothing as stressful and potentially dangerous as working when you are sleep-deprived. Not only is your

productivity affected, but you can also make costly mistakes. You may then have to work even more hours to make up for these mistakes.

- *Seek professional help*
  Everyone needs help from time to time. If your life feels too chaotic to manage and you are spinning your wheels worrying about it, talk with a professional, such as your doctor, a psychologist or a counsellor.

- *Employee Assistance Programmes (EAP)*
  Most good employers provide an EAP. Services provided by your EAP are usually free of charge and confidential. This means no one but you will know what is discussed. If you are experiencing high levels of stress because of marital, financial or work problems, an EAP counsellor can link you to helpful services in your community.

Developing Social Support

Family ties, friendships and involvement in social activities can offer a psychological buffer against stress, anxiety and depression. Social support can also help you cope better with health problems. Cultivating social support can take some effort. Social support is not the same as a support group. Social support is a network of family, friends, colleagues and other acquaintances you can turn to, whether in times of crisis or simply for fun and entertainment. Support groups, on the other hand, are generally more structured meetings or self-help groups, often run by mental health professionals.

Simply talking with a friend over a cup of coffee, visiting with a relative or attending a social group or outing is good for your overall health. Social support can also increase your sense of belonging, purpose and self-worth, promoting positive mental health. You do not necessarily have to actually lean on family and friends for support to reap the benefits of those connections. Just knowing that they are there for you can help you avoid unhealthy reactions to stressful situations. Some people benefit from large and diverse social support systems, while others prefer a smaller circle of friends and acquaintances. In either case, it helps to have people to turn to. That way, someone is always available when you need them, without putting undue demands on any one person. You don't want to wear out your friends!

If you want to expand your social support network, here are some things you can do:

- *Work out*
  Join a class, a local gym or community centre; or start a lunchtime walking group at work.

- *Do lunch*
  Invite an acquaintance to join you for breakfast, lunch or dinner.

- *Volunteer*
  Community groups and other organisations often need volunteers. You can form strong connections when you work with people who share a mutual interest.

- *Join a cause*
  Get together with a group of people working towards a goal you believe in, such as an election or the cleanup of a local park or river.

- *Go back to school*
  Take a college or community education course to meet people with similar interests. Having a variety of interests can create new opportunities to meet people.

- *Maintaining a mutually healthy social support system*
  Developing and maintaining healthy social ties involves give and take. Sometimes you are the one giving support and other times you are on the receiving end. Recognise who is able to provide you with the most support. Letting family and friends know you love and appreciate them will help ensure that their support remains strong when times are rough. Your social support system will help you if you take time to nurture friendships and family relationships. Here are some things to keep in mind:

- *Go easy.* Don't overwhelm friends and family with phone calls or e-mails. Communication can be brief – five minutes on the phone or several sentences in an e-mail. Find out how late or early you can call people and respect those boundaries.
- *Be aware of how others perceive you.* Ask a friend for an honest evaluation of how you come across to others. Take note of any areas for improvement and work on them.
- *Don't compete with others.* This will turn potential friends into potential rivals. The trick is to find people you feel comfortable with rather than those you feel in competition with.

- *Adopt a healthy, realistic self-image*
  Both vanity and rampant self-criticism can be unattractive to potential friends. Accept that you cannot know or do everything. Try to pick balanced people to establish social relationships with.

- *Resolve to improve yourself*
  Cultivating your own honesty, generosity and humility will enhance your self-esteem and make you a more compassionate and appealing person.

- *Avoid relentless complaining*
  Non-stop complaining is tiresome and can be draining on support systems. Talk to your family and friends about how you can change those parts of your life that you are unhappy about.

- *Adopt a positive outlook*
  Try to find the humour in things. When we are stressed we tend to overcomplicate situations and view life as a task. Reframe your view instead thinking about the people and events that you cherish and look forward to.

- *Listen up*
  Make a point to remember what is going on in the lives of others. Then relate any interests or experiences you have in common. Sharing details about yourself and your life can also help establish rapport. The key action is to listen – you may be surprised at what you learn!

Be Wary of Social Support that can Drain you

Some of the people you routinely interact with may be more demanding or harmful than supportive. Give yourself the flexibility to limit your interaction with those people to protect your own psychological well-being. As you seek to expand your social network, be aware of support systems that are unhealthy, oppressive or rigid, or that demand conformity. These can be just as damaging as having no connections at all. In addition, if people in your social support system are continually stressed or ill, you may suffer along with them. If your friends place heavy demands on your time and resources, or if you are unable to meet their needs, you may find yourself more anxious and depressed. You also may pay a psychological toll if you feel obligated to the people in your support network – as if you must continually repay them for their efforts or conform to their beliefs or ideas.

Enjoy Family Time: A Simple Secret

A simple but important secret to spending quality evenings together is to keep the first half-hour you have when you get home from work free of pressure. If one of you is tired and irritable, the other should make a big effort to take care of them. Don't pressure them with questions or make demands. Be gentle and loving. After a hard day trying to stay positive, your partner needs home to be a safe haven. Although it can be difficult, try to make your home a tranquil place where your partner can feel loved and appreciated. It can be tough to create tranquillity in a family home, but consider making your home environment as restful as possible. A vase of flowers on the table or some relaxing music on the stereo can make all the difference when you or your spouse returns home from a busy, stressful world.

Five Final Tips

- *Spend time away*
  Take a long weekend at least four times a year. This weekend is for you and your partner. Not for the children, not for the family, not for solving problems; for no specific purpose other than for

you and your partner to relax. No mobile phone, no e-mail, no computer, no conference calls or 'my work knows how to find me in case of an emergency'; just a long weekend where you are unavailable to everybody except your marriage and your spouse.

- *Life dinner*
  This is a standing date on the first day of every month. Spend the evening talking about the previous month and about the month to come, grounding yourselves in your current reality.

- *Segment space*
  If you work at home, invest in office areas that are clearly separated from the rest of the house. Treat your home as a retreat from the world and, while many people do plenty of working at home, ensure where you do this is separate and distinct from the rest of the house.

- *Be present*
  When at home work hard on being present to your spouse and family. Often if something is troubling us or if we are tired we are not present in the moment.

- *Meditate*
  I use the word meditate metaphorically – everyone should meditate their own way. Some do it while exercising, others while reading. Do whatever you want, but spend some of your time on yourself.

The above habits will create a structure for your life that not only encourages but reinforces a healthy work–life balance. Your work – which used to overwhelm everything else you did – will still be a central part of your life. However, it will no longer be your singular focus, nor will it be the most important thing to you anymore. The balance that you discover will help you understand the value of other things. This will make your work and, more importantly, your family life and marriage much more rewarding.

FINAL WORDS

This book is all about informing you so that you and your spouse can have a happy and long marriage. It is designed to read easily and very quickly give you the knowledge and skills to take control of your life. It is important to reiterate that many of the topics covered are experienced by many if not all marriages. In the modern era it is very hard to create a safe space for love to blossom. Life can often fly by like a Formula One motorcar. It is this speed and the lack of space to reflect and take stock that can send couples into autopilot on the path towards separation and unhappiness. Each chapter in this book gives you the tools and insights to buffer your marriage against this ever-increasing pace.

By examining your family of origin, communication style and how you handle conflict you can begin to learn more about yourself and your spouse. If you as a person are happy and comfortable in your own skin, the challenges of life are easier to surmount. As you become aware of the unhelpful thinking that exists in your mind from childhood and other shortcomings in your worldview you are less likely to fall into conflict. Just as important is the ability to reflect on the qualities that are appreciated and recognised by your family, friends and spouse. During times of pressure, particularly relationship pressure, we sometimes forget the individual traits and qualities that make us special.

Imagine that by reading this book and initiating changes in yourself and your marriage you may be setting up a 'Golden Age' for you, your spouse and your children. A 'Golden Age' is a time of pleasure, comfort and contentment. It is the opposite of walking on eggshells and hoping that things will get better. It is a time when both spouses are happy and balanced, ready for the external slings and arrows that are fired on them from the external world. They are ready because they love each other and realise that they are appreciated and recognised.

Imagine that by reading this book you can break the invisible chains of false perceptions that very often create conflict and toxic anger. You can move away from 'deep-freeze love' to a love that is open and warm and supportive. You can maintain a relationship with your spouse whilst at the same time raising balanced and well-adjusted children. You can accept other people, particularly in-laws, for what they are because you know it comes second to your marriage.

You now understand that emotional connectivity, positive mirroring and absolute honesty are an integral part of marriage. These simple ways of being can help protect your marriage from the trauma of infidelity. You now understand the reasons why marriages fail and have the tools to choose a different path. You realise that work and new technology if not bounded can lead towards stress, hurt and isolation.

The key final action is to choose a new path. Be very clear and set a goal in your mind that you and your spouse now have the knowledge and information to choose this new path. It is not the route of autopilot and hope for the best. Instead it is a conscious effort that, when bedded down in your life, will create happiness. The final ingredient to this is not in this book or within any other person. It is buried firmly within you and is called your personal wisdom. So be wise, take time to reflect on the contents of this book and start creating your own conscious path towards marital bliss.

HELPFUL RESOURCES

If you require further professional help the following organisations are recommended.

ACCORD Marriage Care
A professional and confidential counselling service available to couples throughout Ireland.
Website: www.accord.ie
ACCORD Head Office
Columba Centre, Maynooth College, Kildare
Tel. 01-5053112

Achieve Balance
Professional consultancy on how to restore balance in your life.
Website: www.achievebalance.ie
Tel. 087-2889720

Relate Couple Counselling
Counselling services available throughout the UK and Northern Ireland.
Website: www.relate.org.uk

MRCS
Counselling services available mainly in Dublin area.
Website: www.mrcs.ie
Tel. 1890 380 380

Gamblers Anonymous
Gamblers Anonymous (GA) provides help to people through peer support.
Website: www.gamblersanonymous.ie

BIBLIOGRAPHY

Carnes, P. (1992) *Out of the Shadows: Understanding Sexual Addiction*, Center City, MN: Compcare Publications.

Cooper, J. and Procope, J. (1986) *Seneca Moral and Political Essays*, Cambridge: Cambridge University Press.

De Charms, C. (1993) *A Short History of Buddhism*, London: Oneworld.

Gottman, J. (1994) *Why Marriages Succeed or Fail*, London: Bloomsbury.

Griffiths, Mark (1997) 'Psychology of Computer Use', *Psychological Reports*, Vol. XLIII.

Horvath, A. Hester, R. and Marlatt, A. (1999) *Sex, Drugs, Gambling & Chocolate: A Workbook for Overcoming Addictions*, San Luis Obispo, CA: Impact Publishers.

Kubler-ross, E. (1969) *On Death and Dying*, New York: Touchstone.

Landau, E. (1995) *Hooked: Talking about Addictions*, Brookfield, CT: Millbrook Press.

Mckeown, K. (2002) *Unhappy Marriages, Does Counselling Help?* Maynooth: ACCORD.

Smith, M. and Hazouri, Peyser, S. (1997) *Addiction: The 'High' That Brings You Down*, Hillsdale, NJ: Enslow Publishers.

Stanton, P., Brodsky, A. et al. (1991) *The Truth about Addiction and Recovery*, New York: Simon and Schuster.

Strachey, J. (1966) *Standard Edition of the Complete Works of Sigmund Freud*, London: Hogarth Press.

Woodruff, C. and Gregory, S (2005) 'Profile of Internet Gamblers: Betting on the Future', *UNLV Gaming Research & Review Journal*, Vol. 9, No.1, pp. 1–14.